I0149295

FROM GRIEF TO VICTORY
Looking for a Pony in the Manure Pile

R. P. PALMER

From Grief to Victory
Looking for the Pony in the Manure Pile

ISBN: 978-0-9989363-0-7

Manufactured in the U.S.A.

Cover design by Lisa Hainline (www.lisahainline.com)

Photography by David Shough

Acknowledgments

No endeavor is a one-person operation. God surrounded me with friends and family to help me through difficult times and the writing of this book.

I would like to thank Rodger and Jan Brumbaugh, Steve Campbell, Herb Dias, Rod Hazen, Kim Martin, Tom Parker, Troy Powers, Robert and Gale Smith, Ken Shough, and Dr. William Retts. These people play important roles in my life.

To my friend Dr. Henry Stewart, who assisted me through the process of this manuscript, and Dr. Scott Philip Stewart, the final editor of this writing.

To my mom, Hildred, and my brother, Rodney, who supported me throughout this period in my life.

To the God of the past, present, and future, who truly supplies all of our needs.

Table of Contents

1 – The Early Years

*Listen to me, you islands; hear this, you distant nations:
Before I was born the LORD called me; from my mother's
womb he has spoken my name.*

Isaiah 49:1

Two boys grew up together. Best friends, they were inseparable. They went to the same school, enjoyed the same activities, and spent nearly all their free time with each other. In one way, though, the boys were different: One of the boys saw the positives while the other saw the negatives; one was always optimistic and the other always pessimistic.

Their school principal, who had watched the boys grow up, was so fascinated by their different outlooks that one day she decided to conduct an experiment. Much of the school's landscaping needed fertilizing, and good old-fashioned manure from a local dairy farm was much less expensive than chemical fertilizers. The farmer was ecstatic at the prospect of emptying the cow pen of excess manure and not having to pay for disposal. The school groundskeepers assured the principal they would put all the manure to good use, and since it was the last week of the school year, the smell would not be a problem for the students.

Two days later, a large dump truck deposited the large pile of manure behind the school. The principal, awestruck at the size of the pile, thought, *What are we going to do with all this manure?*

She then moved on to the next phase of her experiment. She summoned the pessimistic boy to her office first. He was probably thinking, *What have I done to deserve being sent to the principal's office?* Then she led him to the manure pile. The boy could see only the mountain of cow exhaust and shrank back at the smell. He wanted nothing to do with this towering mound of dung.

The principal next led the optimistic boy out to the dung heap. He studied the pile for a moment before running to it like a sprinter. Paying no attention to the strong stench, he began digging into the pile like a dog after a buried bone. When the principal asked, "What are you doing?" the boy answered, "There has to be a pony in here somewhere!"

Presented with the same situation, these two boys reacted differently. The results of her experiment did not surprise the principal. Although the boys had grown up in the same neighborhood and had similar backgrounds, they viewed the world around them in very different ways. Why?

We form our view of the world through life experiences. Some come to view the world as a friendly place, some view it as hostile, and some view it as a little of both. The story of the two boys and the pile of manure shows how two people can have different reactions to the same situation. One saw nothing but manure; the other saw the potential of something other than—better than—manure.

A counselor friend shed some light on why people have such differing reactions and views of the world. He said most people develop a world-view in the early years of life. Just as an optometrist writes a prescription for lenses, so life writes a prescription that determines how a person sees the world (that is, his "world-view") before he reaches adolescence. So a child raised in scarcity has a different outlook from a child raised in a more prosperous setting.

We tend to view the messy times of life in two main ways. Are the messes positive or negative? Yes, the manure stinks, but plants thrive on manure fertilizer. Like the pessimistic boy, we can see nothing but manure, or like the optimistic boy, we can see the potential for more than manure. The messy times are often an opportunity to grow. Growing means there is a maturing and a moving forward like a well-nurtured and fertilized plant. Maturing and moving forward are positives in a messy, or negative, setting.

Until the death of my father in 2009, life for me was mostly stable. Earlier that same year God let me know that something difficult was coming in the next few years. He did not tell me exactly *when* it was going to happen. So all I knew was that adversity was coming—that life was about to get messy. I did not anticipate how difficult times would be. It became a lesson of patience and trust, and of wading through piles of manure.

In early 2012, at the beginning of the most trying period of my life, I drew a picture of a pile of manure on a small eraser board on my refrigerator door. Beneath the pile, I wrote the letters **HTMHWTCOI**—an acronym for "**He Told Me He Would Take Care Of It.**" The "He" is God. I was not sure what I was going to experience, but I knew that He would help me through it.

Younger Years

I came into this world at Montgomery Hospital in Ottawa, Illinois, in 1953, a member of the "baby-boomer" generation born in the years after World War II. My dad served in the Navy for seven years before receiving an honorable discharge in 1952. He met my mom not long after he came home from his military service. My mom's family was originally from Kentucky but had moved to northern Illinois and settled in the town where my dad grew up. My parents married in the fall of 1952, and I was born the following summer. A little over two years later, my only sibling, a brother, came into the world.

We lived mainly in small towns and on farms. I remember the milk cows on the farm we lived on when I was about five years old. My dad used a milk separator with a hand crank to separate the cream from the milk. The cream had other uses, such as making butter. My dad had spent many years on a farm in his younger years, which I think is why he chose to return to a life in the country after completing his military service.

Eventually, my dad's work and a desire to move closer to family brought us to Marseilles, Illinois, a small town not far from where I was born. Marseilles is nestled in a part of the Illinois River Valley bordered by the Illinois River on the south and large sandstone bluffs on the north. My dad was born in Marseilles in a small shingle-sided house.

When we moved there, it was a town of about 6,000 residents. Every evening at 6:00 sharp, the very loud steam whistle at the Nabisco plant sounded from one end of town to the other. The whistle was my cue to be home or suffer the consequences.

Many families in that small town, including my own, had lived there for generations. Most of the children were continuous classmates from grade school on into high school. My dad and mom both attended the same high school, and some of their teachers were still there when I went through.

In 1968, my mom accepted her first teaching job at the high school in Shabbona, Illinois, a small farming community in the north-central portion of the state.

For my brother and me, this was not an easy move. We moved to a small farmhouse a few miles west of Shabbona. We were leaving behind all our friends, a devastating blow. I can remember sitting in the living room of the little farmhouse and crying my eyes out. I was in a foreign land, alone. I knew no one except my immediate family. I could make some friends while attending school, but it was hard to form relationships with the other children. The nearest neighbor was about a quarter mile north of us. The family who lived there had a daughter about my age, but I had no interest in associating with her. The friends I made at school lived miles away. We all lived so far apart and none of us drove. I should say none of us had a license to drive on a public roadway. Long before they were eligible for a driver's license, most farm kids were driving trucks and farm machinery – out of necessity to help with harvesting and other duties around the farm. My parents tried to cushion the move by inviting some of our friends from the previous town to come for a visit. Though this helped, it was just not the same as being in our river valley home. This experience was one of the first that left me with the feeling of deep loss.

Going Back

After my mom finished her first year of teaching, she accepted an offer to teach at the high school in Marseilles. We were going back to the town where our friends and family lived. I cannot remember much about this move "home," but I can safely say I had absolutely no hesitation about going. The time in Shabbona was not all bad, but I never felt I "fit in." It was time to go back to where I knew I fit in.

I was back in school with my lifelong friends. My mom was my sophomore English teacher. I do not know who was more uncomfortable, my mom or me. Mom made sure she showed no favoritism toward me. I was a bit of a class clown, but I *had* to behave in her class because if I got in trouble in her class I not only had to face Mom at home but also Dad. For the most part, Mom was an easy touch, but Dad was more of a disciplinarian. The latter is what motivated me to behave in Mom's class.

Moving back was very good for me because my grandfather, one of the most significant influences in my life, lived in Marseilles. Before we moved away, my grandfather and I had spent a lot of time together. He took me hunting and fishing, but most of all he taught me how to live. He was diligent in all he did and never did things halfway. Even when he was well into his 60s, he amazed me with what he could do. For example, he planted and kept an enormous garden. Gardening itself is not so amazing, but he did it all by hand with no power implements. He used hand plows, cultivators, and shovels. His work ethic was the same at home as it was on the job.

My grandfather lived out his beliefs. Sunday was a day of rest, a time to go to church. There was no work, not even any hunting or fishing, on this day. One time I tried to get him to go hunting on a Sunday. He told me the story of a man who went hunting on Sunday. While out hunting, the man tripped over a log and ended up shooting himself. This was his way of telling me that we were not going hunting on Sunday.

If there was a redeeming element in my childhood, it was my grandfather. My dad and I never seemed to connect at an emotional level. My dad would do things with me, but there always seemed to be something lacking in our relationship. I cherish the time I had with my grandfather. My grandfather passed away many years ago, but I reflect often upon the time we spent together.

Moving Again

In 1970, my parents decided to move the family to Arizona. My vision of Arizona included nothing but sand and cactus, which of course is not accurate. The problem was that we moved in July. Summers in the desert areas of Arizona can be blazing hot. Daytime temperatures can exceed 110F (44C), and our vehicle had no air conditioning. Coming from a cooler climate to this inclement heat made the initial experience of Arizona miserable. My parents found a home in Scottsdale, which is where we first settled.

I was then in my late teens. This move to Arizona did not affect me in the same way as the earlier move. Arizona was 1,800 miles away from our home in Illinois, and I am not sure why I did not feel the same about this move.

A few months after moving to Arizona, I was home alone one day when the phone rang. I answered, and the man on the other end asked for my dad. I told him Dad was not there. He then told me that my grandfather had passed away. I was so stunned that I could not speak, and the man had to ask if I was still there. This was my first experience of a death in the family, and although this was not the grandfather I was so close to, it was nevertheless a difficult loss and took some time to process.

My early experiences of church were negative. In our family, going to church was not an option. The churches I recall were very legalistic, meaning they did not allow you to do certain things such as going to movies or bowling or even playing board games that used dice. There was a long list of do's and don'ts. It seemed they were more concerned about outward actions than the inward person. This environment did not foster an attraction to God. If anything, it did just the opposite.

We began to attend a Nazarene church in Scottsdale. One evening, when our family was at the pastor's home, he asked if we wanted to play a game. He got out a Yahtzee game. Now Yahtzee uses dice, and where we came from this was taboo, but evidently it was not taboo in Arizona. I thought, "I think I am going to like it here." I got involved in the church youth group. The church in Scottsdale was very different from the church where we came from—less legalism and more focus on the inner person. This was so very different from my early church experiences.

Even though I was involved in the church youth group, I had not made a total commitment to following Christ. Though I knew how to "act" like a follower of Christ, I had not turned my life over to Him. I am not sure why I was unwilling to commit myself. Maybe it was because I was so leery after my earlier church experiences of legalism. I am sure that had something to do with my disillusionment and reluctance to commit.

How I Met Your Mom

We lived in Scottsdale for about two years before moving to west Phoenix. We remained in contact with one of our neighbors from Scottsdale, Harold, whose wife had lost her battle with cancer. Eventually, Harold began courting a woman he knew who lived in Arkansas. He told me she had a sister, Gladys, and if I wrote her a letter, she would probably write me back. I wrote her and, sure enough, she wrote back. Our correspondence continued for a few months. Harold and Gladys' sister married in early summer of 1973. He invited me to attend the wedding, but I was unable to do so. I did visit Arkansas in July of that year to meet Gladys in person for the first time.

Our initial meeting went well. We went to dinner and then bowling. During my stay in Arkansas, we went to a fireworks stand in a nearby town. People put their names in a bucket for a drawing to win free fireworks. The person at the fireworks stand asked Gladys if she would draw a name from the bucket. She did, and drew my name! What were the chances of her picking my name out of all the names in that bucket? Maybe it was fate; I do not know. What I did know is that we had a good time together during my visit. After I returned to Arizona, Gladys and I continued our correspondence, and I called her about once a week.

In November of 1973, my supervisor handed me a layoff notice. As soon as I read it, I knew what I was going to do. I was going to Arkansas to see Gladys. So, at 20 years old, I loaded up my 1969 baby blue Ford pickup and headed east. Gladys did not know I was coming. I made my weekly call to her from a hotel room so she would not suspect anything. The following day I showed up at her doorstep, and she was surprised to see me.

I spent Thanksgiving and Christmas with Gladys and her family. I had another surprise for Gladys; I brought an engagement ring with me. I decided to wait until Christmas to ask her to marry me. When the right moment came I asked her, and she said "Yes." We made plans for our wedding. She was going to move to Arizona where we were to be married.

In July of 1974, I received a letter from Gladys explaining how she had gone to a tent revival at a local Baptist church and accepted Christ into her life. I knew then that it was time for me to get serious about my relationship with Christ. One evening while alone in my bedroom, I knelt by my bed and asked Christ into my life.

The following month Gladys and I were married in a small church service. Considering neither of us had a job at the time, it was probably not the optimal scenario for two young newlyweds.

Get a Job

I was an unemployed construction worker, which did not impress the in-laws. My mother-in-law expressed her feelings in a letter she sent me before the wedding. Though I tried to assure her that all would be well, I am not sure that did much to allay her concerns. If my daughter was about to marry someone with no job I'm sure I would feel the same way.

As far back as my high school days, I can remember wanting to be a police officer. I am not sure what sparked that desire. During the first year of our marriage, I applied with several police departments in the Phoenix area. In the meantime, I worked temporary jobs doing anything from construction work to warehouse inventory.

In May of 1975, I received a call from the Phoenix Police Department. The man on the phone asked me if I still wanted to be a cop. My answer was a resounding "Yes!" After completing the testing process, I entered the police academy in July. Remember what I said about Arizona in July? We ran daily in the furnace-like heat. On some days, we ran both morning and afternoon.

That fall I graduated from the police academy. My first assignment was in the south Phoenix area. The night of my third shift, the senior officer let me drive. Looking back, I wonder if he knew what was going to happen that night? We ended up chasing a homicide suspect who had just shot someone. We were the third police car in the pursuit. The suspect kept doing U-turns and trying everything to avoid capture. We finally caught him, but I think I almost gave the senior officer a heart attack in the process. This was the beginning of many such experiences during my years in police work.

Ten years later, my career was doing well but my marriage was not. By this time, we had two young daughters, a mortgage, and two vehicles. We went to church every Sunday and were involved in church activities. Though on the exterior everything looked good, the situation on the inside was anything but good. In fact, something was drastically wrong between Gladys and me. We argued constantly. I tried to figure out why we were not getting along and concluded that it must be my job. Police work is notoriously difficult for spouses and families. One of the main reasons police work takes a toll on families is that there is always the potential that the officer could be hurt or killed.

Ten years into my dream job, I resigned to save my marriage. My marriage and family were a higher priority to me. I went to work with my dad, who was a contractor who did home repairs and remodeling. I like doing this sort of work, but working with my dad was stressful. He had a rigid way of doing the work, and there was no deviating from his way of doing things. When I do a job, I look at different ways to complete a task. Normally, I pick the path of least resistance. This is where my dad and I differed, and it created even more tension in an already tense, difficult relationship.

In the months after I left the police department, my relationship with Gladys improved slightly, but there remained a void in our marriage. Our relationship never got past the superficial, and she acted as if she did not wish to connect at a deeper level. To this day, I do not know why. By this time, we were about 12 years into our marriage. One would think that, 12 years in, a marriage would be past the superficial stage.

After working with my dad for several months, I decided to go to refrigeration school. It was a six-month program and a good trade in this part of the country because air conditioning is a necessity for those living in the desert. After completing refrigeration school, I continued working with my dad. The air conditioning training helped on some of the jobs we did together and was a source of extra income for me.

As with any kind of contracting work, it was "feast or famine." At times, we were overwhelmed with work, and at other times, there was scarcely any work. We had a tight family budget. Gladys worked outside the home, but we needed two steady paychecks for financial stability. I needed a more stable income. After an 18-month hiatus from the police department, I applied to go back. After I was rehired, I continued to do air conditioning jobs on the side to supplement the household income. Our marriage was doing better, but I felt there was still something lacking. There was a schism between us that appeared unbridgeable. The question was: "What was the cause of this schism?"

To Think About:

1. Who were the people who influenced you the most in your younger years? How did they influence your life?

2. What are your earliest memories of losses? Do you remember how you dealt with them?

3. Do you have strained relationships with a parent or close family member? Can you reestablish these relationships?

2 – The Call

His divine power has given us everything we need for a godly life through our knowledge of him who called us by his own glory and goodness.

2 Peter 1:3

One morning in late 1999, as I was reading and praying before I left the house to go to work, I heard the Lord telling me He wanted me to be a police chaplain. Though I did not hear an audible voice, it was clear what I had heard. My initial response was, "You want me to do what?" I had no intention of going into the ministry. I was content working and going to church. Yet I knew that if this message was truly from the Lord, He would take care of everything. When God instructs someone to do something, He provides direction and a means to accomplish it. My part was obedience and doing what He wanted me to do. This was my "call" to ministry.

Prior to my encounter that morning, I had started taking college classes "for fun." I was not serious and was not even sure if I would complete a bachelor's degree program. After hearing from God, however, I knew it was time to apply serious effort to my studies. In my view, I needed a good education to do ministry well. Most pastors I knew had a graduate seminary degree. If I were to eventually enroll in seminary, I would need an undergraduate degree.

I attended evening classes several nights a week. Many nights I would stop by a friend's house, eat quickly, take a short nap on the sofa, and then head to class. Some classes finished as late as 9:00 PM. After driving home, I would crawl into bed for a few hours of sleep and then start work the next day at 7:00 AM.

This routine of working full-time and attending school at night continued for three years. When I went fishing or camping, I often took school material with me. At times, I sat in the shade of a tree to study. This was an ideal study environment for me – a peaceful environment with no interruptions. I could read or write devoid of any interference from a phone or pager and even sneak in an occasional nap if I wished.

In December of 2001, a retired sergeant I knew from the Phoenix Police Department gave me a call. He had become a police chaplain in a city east of Phoenix. He told me about an area police department seeking a chaplain and recommended that I speak to the chief of the department about the opening. I knew the chief because we had worked together in Phoenix, so I called him and we agreed to meet to discuss the chaplain position.

Before I met with the chief, I decided that if he asked me to serve as chaplain, I would retire from the Phoenix Police Department. If he offered me the position, I would see it as the door God was opening for me to begin my police chaplain ministry. If he did not offer me the position, I would see that as God's doing, too, and stay with the police department at least another five years before retiring.

What do chaplains do? I wondered. Do they sit around looking like Moses who just came down from the mountaintop with some stone tablets? Do they act like some spiritual guru? I had never dealt with any of the chaplains who worked with the police department when I was in Phoenix. I had occasion to speak with them at different times but never on a "professional" level. When I needed to speak to someone, I sought out people from my church. I never asked a chaplain about his duties. I knew they performed weddings and funerals and apparently did the same things as a minister of a church. The difference was that the chaplain's congregation consisted of police officers.

The following January, the police chief and I met for lunch. During our conversation, he asked me when I wanted to start. I told him I needed to work until March to complete 25 years of service, and he agreed to let me start then.

March 20, 2002 was my last day on the Phoenix police force. I went to the retirement office a week or so before my actual retirement date to sign the retirement papers, which was a stack so thick I wondered if I was buying a house. After receiving my final paperwork from the city, a group of us met at a local restaurant for my farewell luncheon. All I wanted was to have lunch with some of my closer colleagues; that would suffice for me. What made the day special was being with those with whom I had known and served alongside for many years. Earlier that day, I received a phone call from one of the assistant police chiefs with whom I had worked many years earlier. He asked if he could attend and came and presented me with a retirement plaque.

Leaving my job of 25 years behind was not as difficult as I thought it might be. Sure, I would miss the people I had known for years, but I knew that I was doing what the Lord wanted me to do. Instead of being sad over my departure, I had a sense of excitement about moving on.

Now What?

The old cliché "Like a fish out of water" summarizes how I felt. I was way out of my known element of the past 25 years. Making the shift from police officer to police chaplain was a challenge. I was around police officers, but now I was their "chaplain." I knew all the police lingo and how to be a police officer. Though I knew I was in the right place because of the timing and sequence of events that had brought me to that juncture, I was at a loss about what I was supposed to do. I had no one to mentor me, no one to train me in the "how to" of being a chaplain. At that time, I did not know other police chaplains. The police department's policy book defined some of the duties expected of a chaplain, but it did not address the day-to-day activities of a chaplain. My only option was to get started. So that's what I did. Sitting around contemplating what I was going to do or was supposed to do would not get me anywhere.

During my first year as a chaplain, I spent much of my time building relationships and trust with the people. Once people trust each other, a true relationship can grow. Sharing deep issues and concerns does not occur until mutual trust is in place. Though it took some time, that is exactly what happened. My prior police service helped me gain the officers' trust and build relationships, which opened doors for ministering to them. Police officers are a very close group of individuals. They depend upon one another daily in life-and-death situations. Those who have not performed the job cannot truly understand the unique challenges of police officers, despite their best efforts. With 25 years of service on the blue line, I was able to access these officers' lives and counsel them personally when they requested help.

After serving as a chaplain for a little over a year, I had the chance to attend a one-week police and prison chaplain training. The training I received was a great help, and the people I met there became helpful resources for my chaplaincy. Steve Lee, the founder of Police Officer Ministries, became one of my initial mentors.

In the fall of 2003, one of the police lieutenants developed stomach problems. He was in his early 40s and very physically fit so the doctors initially believed an ulcer was the most likely culprit. I had witnessed him chastising officers for their tobacco use on more than one occasion. The issue with his stomach was serious enough to warrant a hospital stay. Gladys and I went to visit him, and he was very positive and had an excellent prognosis.

He did not respond to their treatment, and the doctors eventually diagnosed him with leukemia. This came as a shock to everyone. He underwent treatments for months and had multiple hospital stays. I had a dream about the lieutenant in May of 2004. In this dream, I saw that he would not survive his illness. I have had dreams like this in the past, very vivid dreams that I can remember in detail. It was Sunday morning, and instead of going to church I went to the hospital to visit the lieutenant. As a Christian minister, I wanted to make sure he was spiritually ready to meet God when he passed away. When I met with him, he told me that everything was in God's hands.

A month later, I was at the hospital one evening. By then it was apparent to everyone that he would not survive. But although he was unconscious, the lieutenant kept hanging onto life. His wife approached me and asked what I thought about her plan. She wanted to have the whole family go into his room and say their goodbyes. Then, after they left, the young woman who played music for the patients on the oncology floor would come into the room and play her guitar and sing for him, which the lieutenant enjoyed. I told the lieutenant's wife that it sounded like a good plan.

So the family gathered in the room and said their goodbyes. When they left the room, the young woman went in and closed the door. I stood outside the door. A few minutes later, the door opened, and the tears streaming down the young woman's face told us that the lieutenant had passed away. One of the lieutenant's sisters began to cry uncontrollably. I led her into a nearby room and left her with some of her family members.

What I did next was one of the most difficult things I have ever done in my life. I walked down to a waiting room full of police officers to inform them that their friend had passed away. The short walk to that room seemed like it took an eternity. I tried to formulate what I was going to say when I got there, without crying myself. When I got to the room, all I could squeak out was, "He's gone." Then I left those officers sitting there in grief and went back to the room to be with the family.

Experiencing the loss of the lieutenant was difficult for all of us at the police department. His death was a painful reminder of the brevity of life. Many kept a small photograph of the lieutenant at their workstations long after he passed away. This was an indicator of the impact he had on those around him. Some of us may never know the impact or the influence we have in this world. I suspect the lieutenant had not understood his influence on those around him. One of his favorite sayings was, "I'll die for you but I won't lie for you." He was indeed a man of great integrity. So, although he was gone, he remained alive in the hearts of those who knew him.

The loss of someone like this—a healthy, vibrant devoted family man in his 40s—is one of life's worst-case scenarios. He left behind a wife, two teenage children, and a loving family. He and his wife were childhood sweethearts and no doubt expected they would grow old together. And now he was gone, struck down in the prime of life, way too soon. How can anyone find a pony in this manure pile?

I have observed parents who lost a child. I do not think any parent can recover fully from the loss of a child, no matter how old the child is. The death of a child before a parent is simply not the natural order. No parent should ever have to bury a child. The initial shock of death subsides with time, but the void of the one who is gone remains forever.

A Christian couple I know lost their son when he was 17 years old. He spent his days confined to a wheelchair because he suffered from a pulmonary condition. I cannot recall a time I ever saw this young man without a smile on his face. He was always cheerful. He refused to let the circumstance dictate his identity. One day he could barely breathe. His mother drove him to the doctor, but the efforts to save him failed and he passed away.

Although his parents grieved profoundly, there was something different about their grief. Some parents do not recover from losses like this. Some marriages do not survive losses like this. So why was their grief different from that of other parents who have lost children? It was different because of their faith in God. They knew that when their son departed our world, he entered Heaven to be with a loving God where there is no more pain or suffering. These are the promises of God, a firm foundation these parents can stand on during their time of loss. Eventually, their tears did turn to smiles even though I know there will remain an empty spot in their hearts due to their son's absence until they meet with him again in Heaven when he is healthy and all is as it should be.

To see their pony in this manure pile took time. For anyone to see the pony in situations like this could take years. Remember one thing: God is not on our timetable. It takes time to recover from any loss. Be assured that God is with you and that there is a "pony" in store for you at the appointed time.

Taking a Break

I received my bachelor's degree in the fall of 2002. I considered starting seminary but decided to take a year off. Taking a break would give me time to concentrate on ministry and catch up with things I had not done for a long time. I knew that going to seminary would not only benefit me but those I serve as well.

When I began to consider seminaries I restricted my search to the Phoenix area because my family lived here and my ministry base is in the area. I examined two seminaries and chose Fuller Southwest in Phoenix.

In the fall of 2003, I started the seminary coursework. I took one class at a time to avoid a crushing burden of school debt. Seminary programs usually run three years. I completed my coursework in seven years. I was in no hurry to finish even though other students were graduating and I still had more coursework ahead of me.

Not long after I began seminary, a friend asked me to officiate his daughter's wedding. This would be the first wedding ceremony I ever performed. Just the thought of getting up in front of a group of people made me cringe. I reluctantly said "Yes" even though the butterflies in my stomach were saying "No." I survived officiating my first wedding with no problems. The butterflies have gotten smaller after numerous weddings since.

When I first began my ministry as a chaplain, my frustration level was high. I think part of it was self-induced because I was new and adjusting to being a chaplain. Working with people frustrated me because I had their best interests at heart. Some did not listen no matter how hard I tried to help them. I finally learned that I could not do the work of God. I can present God and His Word to people but they are free to respond however they wish. Their response is not up to me. I am only the messenger. Once I learned this, my frustration diminished. This lesson was the pony in the manure pile of my own frustration.

In seminary, I learned that a pastor has two tools – a washbasin and a towel. These are what Jesus used to wash His disciples' feet (John 13). Why did Jesus do this? Was it due to a lack of hygiene on the part of the disciples? No, Jesus was teaching His disciples a valuable lesson in how His followers are to serve others. Jesus knew His time on earth was short, and He was teaching His disciples how to humble themselves. Jesus, God in human form, washing the feet of these men. This was a supreme act of love. The Creator humbling Himself before men. Anyone who claims to follow Jesus needs to grasp this and practice it.

We all have a call to ministry. It doesn't matter whether you are a senior pastor or a janitor. We all serve in the ways God sees fit. Never downplay where God has placed you. You are there for a purpose. You are one of many parts of the Body of Christ, the body of believers. If God the Creator humbled Himself in human form, washed the feet of men, then who are we? Never lose sight of who you are in God's eyes.

Those in ministry and those claiming to follow Jesus need to confront themselves at the level these disciples were. Peter, for instance, told Jesus he would not let Him wash his feet. Peter thought this act of foot washing was something too menial for Jesus. Jesus told Peter, "Unless I wash you, you have no part with me" (John 13:8). When Jesus said this to Peter, he then let Him wash his feet. There is a significant parallel in this story. Jesus' washing the disciples' feet represents what Jesus can do with an unclean heart and life. No matter how messed up a person thinks his or her life is, Jesus can change what is unclean into what is clean.

Jesus' washing the disciples' feet goes against human nature. It takes the love of Jesus manifested in a person to humble oneself to wash the feet of others. Only one who is in true relationship with Jesus can comprehend what He did with His disciples. The question followers of Jesus need to ask themselves is: "Am I willing to wash the feet of others?" If not, why not?

To Think About:

1. How do you know God is asking you to do something? How willing are you to follow His requests?

2. Each of us has a limit to what we will do for God. Where is your limit? Have you ever pushed that limit?

3. Put yourself in Peter's place. Do you think you would let Jesus wash your feet or would you react as Peter did?

3 – The Church Plant and My Father

Since no one knows the future, who can tell someone else what is to come?

Ecclesiastes 8:7

After I retired from the police department, Gladys and I moved to a rural area 20 miles west of Phoenix. The thing I enjoy most about living away from the city is the quietness. We hear a siren from time to time, but for the most part it is peaceful. Yet we were 21 miles away from our home church in Phoenix.

We began attending that church in the early 1990s. Our children grew up there, and many of our friends attended. The church building was in a neighborhood of sprawling horse farms, a fine setting for the church. Jake, the senior pastor, was well-suited as the leader. The pastor and the people were like family to us, and it was the best church we had ever attended.

A few years later, Jake was appointed overseer of all the denomination's churches in Arizona in addition to serving as our pastor. This change meant he would be his own boss because he was both the overseer and a pastor. Jake's superior lived out of state and saw him face-to-face possibly six times per year. So who would hold Jake accountable since his boss only saw him a few times a year? This situation had the potential for disaster.

We saw some issues developing within the church and knew they were not right. Jake appointed people to the church board who would say "yes" to his requests. So nearly every issue Jake favored that came to a vote passed. The church board minutes confirmed those suspicions because the same people always made the motions and seconded them.

Over time, I saw changes in Jake. He was not the same person I met when we began attending the church. To be honest, I thought he was becoming a jerk and losing any pastoral ability in dealing with people. I observed a counseling session Jake conducted and could not believe how poorly he treated the man he was counseling. He did not go to church and was seeking help from a pastor. Jake intentionally made the man mad so he would not come back. This man was not a Christian, and after that session and how poorly he was treated I doubt seriously that he would ever consider being one. This was the first time I saw Jake treat someone in this manner. The bullying approach became one of the primary "tools" he used to get rid of anyone who opposed him.

I began to question whether Jake could be trusted after observing his conduct. As a police officer, I had developed a "sixth sense" about many situations, and what I sensed about Jake was not good. My respect and trust for him diminished significantly after what I observed.

Jake began hiring church staff members he could control, including associate and youth pastors. Most of the people he hired could not be trusted. Those who could be trusted either left after a short time or were fired by Jake.

I faced a serious dilemma. The denomination paid a portion of my seminary tuition. If I did not remain with the denomination for five years, I would have to repay part of the money. So I could not afford to leave because I would have to pay back thousands of dollars. I had no other choice but to remain with the denomination and hope everything worked out.

The Church Plant

The denomination had made two previous attempts to start a church near where we lived. Neither succeeded. In late 2006, they made plans to try a third time. The funding and effort levels were much higher this time. Jake appointed a man named Pete and his wife as the pastors to lead the church planting. We knew Pete and his wife and thought they would be a great pastoral team. Gladys and I joined the church planting group because it was much closer to our home. We had never been part of a project like this and it gave us an opportunity to distance ourselves from Jake.

By February 2007, we were ready to begin. Twenty people attended the first service that we held in the family room of Pete's home. The planned space at a local high school was not yet ready.

We saw steadily increasing attendance over the first year. Meanwhile, however, Pete was becoming concerned because he had caught Jake in several lies. This bothered him so much that he was considering raising the issue with the denomination's regional board. I didn't think this was a good idea because it would put Pete's job and the church plant in jeopardy.

At a church plant retreat in February of 2008, Pete again mentioned that he would confront Jake. I should have tried to dissuade Pete at the time, but I did not. He made up his mind to take the grievances he had against Jake to the regional board.

Afterwards, Pete followed through with his confrontation of Jake in front of the regional board. Pete leveled serious charges of misconduct against Jake, which of course displeased the pro-Jake board. Pete had poked the proverbial hornets' nest.

When I learned about Pete's actions, I sent an email to the church planting team expressing concerns. We had put a lot of work into that church plant, but given what had transpired I knew it faced an uncertain future. In my email, I said the group should be involved before someone made "a decision of this magnitude" that affected the whole. Nothing could change what Pete had done. All we could do at that point was wait to see what would happen next.

After Pete received my email, he told me that we had discussed the situation while we were at the retreat. I had considered our conversation a statement of what he was going to do rather than a discussion.

Jake called me to set up a meeting but he did not tell me what it was about. When we met he told me that he was terminating Pete. He asked me to take over as pastor of the church plant. I told him that I had not yet completed seminary, was still a chaplain with the police department, and could not take on any further responsibilities. What I did not tell Jake was that after observing his actions, I was not willing to subject myself to his unethical standards. I don't think Jake liked it that I was turning down his request, but I simply did not feel comfortable taking the position.

The tension was high on Pete's last Sunday. People were upset to see him and his wife leave, especially under the circumstances. We had worked hard together and experienced great sadness seeing it end. The goodbyes and going our separate ways was painful and difficult.

In the Interim

We needed a replacement pastor, and Jake appointed a woman named Cathy as interim pastor. She was a good choice. She and her husband lived 90 miles away but were willing to drive the distance on a continuing basis. Everything was going well for the first month. For reasons known only to Jake, however, Cathy did not remain as the pastor even after we requested that she stay. Though I never learned the precise reason, I suspect Jake fired Cathy because she did not fit the type of pastor he preferred.

Mortimer, the next pastor Jake appointed, had been attending the church with his wife and children. Though he did not have pastoral training, he was a good communicator. No one was sure what he would be like as a pastor, but we were willing to give him a chance.

In a few Sundays, we knew Mortimer's true nature. Every week he preached "You're going to Hell" type sermons. They reminded me of the sermons I heard as a young man. People suggested that he change his single-sermon subject, but he would not listen. We heard the same topic every Sunday: hellfire and brimstone.

On the Sunday before Memorial Day 2008, Mortimer preached on the sacrifices made by those who have died for this country. He did well until he said, "How many of them went to Hell?" My dad, a Korean War veteran visiting that Sunday, did not appreciate that comment. This was supposed to be a day to honor veterans, not wonder how many of them went to Hell! The sermon upset people, and they again told Mortimer that he needed to change the theme of his sermons. Yet he continued his single-minded focus on Hell-themed messages.

On Fathers' Day, Mortimer delivered the morning sermon and shocked everyone at its end. He announced to the congregation that this was to be his last Sunday, and then he and his family walked out. The congregation sat there in disbelief. I stood up and followed Mortimer outside. He told me, "These people do not want to have church; all they want is a social club." He and his family got in their car and left. Mortimer was the type of pastor Jake hired. They would listen to and obey Jake without question. Mortimer was the one who did not listen to sound advice and then blamed the congregation for his own actions. This was an example of the way Jake operated; he shocked people and left before they could respond.

Jake called a meeting of what was left of the church plant team the Monday following Mortimer's departure. When Gladys and I arrived, we saw Jake and two other "horsemen of the apocalypse" – Don and Harry – getting out of a vehicle. We knew that the three together were not bringing good news to us. Don and Harry were part of the pro-Jake regional board who would consent to anything Jake wanted. I asked myself why it took three of them to invade the meeting.

Jake started the meeting and did most the talking. He told us that we had done a good job with the church plant. Then, in typical Jake blindsiding fashion, he told us that he was "pulling the plug" on the plant. This was reminiscent of the tactic Mortimer had used the previous morning in church. It was Jake's usual hit-and-run tactic, dropping the bombshell of dire news and then leaving before anyone had time to process and respond to the news. After Jake finished the carpet-bombing, the three got back on their "horses" and left us sitting in a daze. By "pulling the plug," Jake meant we would receive no more financial support from the denomination.

It became obvious that Mortimer had demonized us because we did not approve of his single-sermon approach. I think he presented us to Jake as a group of malcontents because we did not mindlessly follow him.

When we began to recover, we discussed our options and next steps. We agreed that we were not ready to abandon the project. Renaldo, another pastor in the denomination, was part of the church plant. We decided that Renaldo and I would continue as the pastors.

The next day, I called Jake with the plan. He agreed to let us continue but on the condition that we would receive no denominational funding.

There was a hint of a pony in this pile of manure because Jake said we could continue using the equipment from the church plant.

The rental contract with the high school was expiring shortly, and the size of our group did not justify staying at the high school. The church my parents attended did not have Sunday evening service, so I contacted their pastor and worked out a rental agreement, and we moved out of the high school.

We needed a music leader but could not find one despite a thorough search. Then Gladys received an email from a couple in a church in our denomination about 90 miles away volunteering to lead music. I was amazed that someone 90 miles away would volunteer to help with the music, and we did not hesitate to accept their offer. This was another glimpse of a pony in the pile.

Starting Again

Renaldo and I alternated preaching every other Sunday. He worked full-time, and I was busy with chaplaincy and school. I took the first Sunday with 15 of the original group in attendance. Our Sunday evening attendance remained the same size. Though we worked to increase our attendance, it was difficult to get people to come on Sunday evenings.

A month after we took over the church plant, doctors discovered my dad had two aneurysms in his chest and abdominal area. These conditions were serious enough to require surgery to repair them because either one could rupture at any time and he would not survive.

It took two months for my dad to get approval for the surgery for only one of the aneurysms. He had surgery in the latter part of October, four months after the aneurysms were discovered. The surgery went well, and there were no suspected complications. After a short stay in Intensive Care, the hospital transferred him to a regular room. Everything was going better than expected.

The hospital was a 40-minute drive from my parent's home, too far away to make several trips a day. We decided that the best option was to go to the hospital in the morning and return home in the evening. My mom and I began the long days at the hospital, arriving in the morning and staying well into the evening.

My dad has a severe issue with vertigo and if he lies on his left side he begins vomiting. The white board in his hospital room had the instructions written on it, "**Do not lay on left side; patient gets vertigo.**"

One morning before we arrived at the hospital, someone who had obviously not seen the warning written on the board in his room rolled dad onto his left side, and he became violently ill. When we arrived at the hospital, I did not go directly to the room but mom did. A doctor and a nurse were in the room behind the closed curtain around his bed. Mom could hear him gagging because the doctor was attempting to insert a tube down his throat. This went on for several minutes until my mom had heard enough. She flung the curtain open and stood there glaring at the doctor and nurse. No words were exchanged, but I can picture a hint of fire coming from my mom's eyes. The doctor received the message my mom was sending, and he and the nurse left the room.

I am not sure why the doctor was trying to insert that tube. Maybe he thought they would relieve something by inserting a tube into his stomach. What I do know is that this incident caused a major setback in his recovery. This was a heartbreaking turn of events. Everything was going so well until then. What was supposed to be a few-day stay in the hospital had become a question of whether he was ever going to get out of the hospital. His condition deteriorated, his skin began to turn a yellowish color, and his overall condition was poor.

My dad's condition was a cause of great concern. I was eight months away from my seminary graduation and wanted both of my parents to see me graduate. I prayed and asked God to let my dad be there to see me graduate.

The next morning, Mom and I made the daily trip to the hospital. What we witnessed when we got to Dad's room was miraculous. He was sitting on the edge of his bed. The yellowish color of his skin was gone, and he said, "I got to get out of here." I knew God had answered my prayer. There was no other explanation for the sudden change in his condition, and shortly thereafter he was released from the hospital.

His recovery was slow. Dad loved to work outside and was constantly finding projects around the house to keep him busy. I could see the surgery had taken a toll because he could no longer work for long periods as he once could.

One day as Dad and I were sitting at the dining room table at my parent's home, he remarked, "I'm tired." Those words coupled with the look on his face told me what he was trying to say. He was telling me that he was ready to leave this life. Those words were difficult for me to digest.

To Think About:

1. How do you view the church? Is it relevant in today's world?

2. Do you or would you feel comfortable attending a church? What, if any, are your apprehensions about it?

3. If you were in a situation like the one with Jake, how would you handle it? Would you stay and confront him? Would you leave? Would you stay and "ride it out"?

4 – Revelation and the Days Ahead

Your relatives, members of your own family— even they
have betrayed you; they have raised a loud cry against
you. Do not trust them, though they speak well of you.
Jeremiah 12:6

During the first week of April 2009 I awoke after a vivid dream like the one I had before the lieutenant passed away. I saw a knife with a broken blade and tried to fix it by putting the two halves of the blade back together. An inaudible voice spoke to me and told me not to fix the blade. I then woke up with a racing heart wondering what that dream meant. I told Gladys about it, and we both decided that maybe it was telling me not to reconcile with Jake.

The following night I had another dream in which I saw one of the police officers I worked with in the mid-1980s holding a pistol in his right hand. In the foreground, two girls were kneeling and hugging each other. The officer raised the pistol, and then I woke up to the sound of a car horn. An inaudible voice told me that this officer is the one Gladys had an affair with 25 years earlier. The voice said, "Divorce her." I replied, "This happened so long ago there is no way I can prove it." The voice said, "I will take care of it." That day I prayed "if this is true, please tell me it's true." God hates divorce, and I was looking for affirmation. I needed to know without a doubt that this was what *God* was telling me to do.

The next night I awoke again at the same time. The inaudible voice said, "It's true." This was the affirmation I sought, erasing any uncertainty.

I had never experienced three consecutive nights like this before. The broken knife blade represented my marriage. The dream told me not to attempt to "fix" my marriage. The second night gave the reason I was not to "fix" my marriage. Several months passed before God revealed the meaning of the two girls in the dream. They represented the double life Gladys was living – the faithful churchgoer and the unfaithful wife. I never told Gladys about the second and third dreams and just kept those revelations to myself.

The dreams answered questions I had pondered for many years. The officer in my dream was a former partner who had worked and ridden with me. One morning my sergeant told me that my partner no longer wanted to ride with me. He offered me no explanation. After the dream, I realized that this coincided with the time when the officer and Gladys were having an affair.

For many years, I tried to get Gladys to go to marriage counseling, but she was not interested. One time six years before I had those dreams, Gladys and I were driving to Kingman, Arizona. I mentioned to her that we could start looking at ways to improve our marriage. Her reply was, "Can't we just drive?" On another occasion, when I suggested we go to counseling she replied, "Only if the kids go." This made absolutely no sense to me since our daughters were adults and did not live with us. After this exchange, I never mentioned counseling or improving our marriage again. Her refusal to work on our marriage made more sense to me after the dreams. I believe she was afraid that her indiscretion would come to the surface and chose instead to keep it hidden. Another missing piece of the puzzle was now in place.

After that revelation about Gladys, I began to question if there was *anyone* I could rely upon. I did not trust the leadership in my church because of what Jake had done. Now, I could no longer trust my wife because of what she had done. The two places that should be sanctuaries of faithfulness had become houses of betrayal. I could not place confidence either in the leadership of my church or in my wife. "Who could I trust?" This question left me feeling confused and disillusioned. The people in my life I confided in were all suspect. Though I knew God is always faithful and trustworthy, the number of people I could rely upon was dwindling.

I felt angry and betrayed by my wife. I did not confront her about the affair because God said, "I will take care of it." Even if I had confronted her, she would have lied about it. After all those years of hiding what she had done, she was not going to come clean suddenly. All I could do was wait on God to do what He said He was going to do. How long would I have to wait? That would rest with God and His plan and timetable.

What Next?

On June 13, 2009, God answered my prayer in allowing both my parents to attend my seminary graduation ceremony. Less than a week after graduation, however, my life was about to undergo a drastic redirection.

Gladys' car needed an oil change and I started early to avoid the heat of the day. Before I finished, my mom called and left a message asking me to call her. When I returned her call a few minutes later, she told me that something was wrong with dad. He was experiencing severe pain in his back and his efforts to relieve the pain were unsuccessful. I finished the oil change and went to my parents' house. Dad was in such severe pain that we decided we needed to take him to the hospital.

The ER doctor ordered a computerized tomography (CT) scan. While we were waiting for the results of the scan, I called my brother and the pastor of my parents' church to apprise them of the situation. The scan revealed that my dad's remaining aneurysm was leaking and that a rupture would likely be fatal.

The hospital was not equipped to perform the emergency surgery so they called for a helicopter to transport him to a facility in Phoenix. My brother arrived at the hospital just as it was landing. When Mom and I arrived at the hospital, Dad was already in surgery, and it continued until evening.

In the recovery room, his body was so swollen from the fluids they had given him that we hardly recognized him. Our visits were brief because he was not aware of our presence. The surgeon told us it was now a matter of waiting.

I knew the situation with my dad was not good, so I spoke with Renaldo about the future of the church plant. I did not know how long dad was going to be in the hospital. My mom no longer drove, and I was going to be the one taking her to the hospital. I would not be able to continue with the church plant for a time, meaning Renaldo would need to handle all the duties in my absence. He did not want to continue alone, however, so we agreed it was time to quit. Though it was not an easy decision after all we had invested in the plant, it was the *right* decision. Our two-year church planting adventure thus came to an end.

The Long Days

For the next 16 days, Dad was in ICU on a ventilator and sedated. He was never able to communicate while in ICU because of the sedation. During the day, we made short visits to his room but spent most of the day in the waiting area.

In our daily trips to the hospital, we left home at 8:30 AM and did not return until 9:00 or 10:00 PM. There was no other option because the hospital was too far away to be making trips back and forth during the day. We spent Father's Day in the hospital. I had bought a gift for Dad before he went into the hospital. I took it to the hospital and left it in his room hoping that eventually I could give it to him.

While Dad was in the hospital, I had another dream, at the same time of night as the other ones. I saw a small television on a dresser with no picture and only a snowy screen. While looking at the television screen, I turned to my left and saw a clear window with no curtain. It was dark outside, a cold and flawlessly clear winter night. One bright star stood out among all the others. While I looked at the stars, the bright star suddenly disappeared. Then an inaudible voice said, "He is not going to make it." This was a forewarning of what was to come. My dad was not going to survive, and God was preparing me for the loss. Even with this warning of what was to come, I did not know how to process this revelation. Knowing that he was not going to survive did not alleviate the emotion of the day. If anything, it made it worse. Now, I would be watching from the sideline waiting for that moment to come. It was not a matter of *if* it was going to happen only of *when* it was going to happen.

I had known that Dad was not doing well, and this dream just confirmed it. I never shared this dream with my mom. She was so sure that he was going to recover. Though there were times I attempted to tell her that there might be a chance Dad may not survive, but she just did not want to believe it.

Getting Transferred

By the beginning of July, Dad had reached a juncture where the hospital in Phoenix could do nothing further for him. We began the process of locating a long-term facility. We checked out several and decided on one in Sun City, closer to home.

On July 6, an ambulance transported Dad to the aftercare facility. By the time the ambulance left the hospital, it was late afternoon rush-hour traffic. Mom and I followed the ambulance as it negotiated through traffic and took alternate routes to get across town as swiftly as possible. My nerves were on edge because Dad was not in the best condition and the ambulance ride was not helping him. I wanted him to get to the facility and complete the transfer. Even when we finally arrived at the long-term facility, the process seemed to take forever, which just added more stress with every hour.

My mom's first exchange with one of the nurses did not go well. My mom asked the nurse if they were going to give dad a diuretic to help rid him of excess fluid. The nurse replied, "No, he is not diabetic." There was an obvious communication issue between that nurse and my mom who of course knew that her husband was not a diabetic; they had been married for 56 years. My mom had reached her limit. Her stress level was at a maximum with all she had been through with Dad in the previous weeks. She and the nurse finally understood one another and settled the issue.

Two doctors – one a pulmonologist and the other, an internist – worked for this facility. When the internist initially examined my dad, he told us, "He does not look good." When the pulmonologist initially examined my dad, he told us, "He's not doing too badly for what he has been through." Which assessment were we to believe? Mom was leaning towards the pulmonologist's assessment while I was leaning towards the internist's assessment.

The medications Dad received appeared to be taking a toll both mentally and physically. The ground-floor room he was in had a large multi-paned window that looked out on a parking lot. Looking out the window revealed only cars and pickup trucks. One day, Dad commented on the ships he saw out the window. We were not sure what he was seeing but thought that maybe he was reverting to his days in the Navy.

One morning I walked into his room and found him with a terrified look on his face. "Call the sheriff," he told me. I said, "Why do you want me to call the sheriff?" He said, "Because they are trying to kill me." He was convinced that the staff had murder on their minds and he was the intended victim. After Mom and I spent some time with him, he calmed down.

Seeing him in this condition was difficult. His toes were turning black. The medication that raised his blood pressure after the surgery contributed to the darkening of the toes. We experienced a sense of helplessness because there was nothing we could do to improve the situation.

A physical therapist was working with my dad and used a machine to hoist him out of bed for therapy sessions. He first had Dad sitting in a chair, then progressed to having him stand, and eventually had him taking a few steps. It appeared that Dad was making progress in his recovery. He was very weak and taking a few steps took great effort. Even though it appeared he was making progress toward recovery, the dream about him remained fresh in my mind.

It was early August then, and one evening when I arrived home after Mom and I had spent another long day at the facility with Dad, Gladys said, "This is getting old." By "this" she was referring to my absence from home while caring for my mom and dad. It was like pouring salt into an open emotional wound. Mom and I were not going to the facility daily for pleasure or enjoyment. We were going out of necessity. I did not respond to Gladys' comment because I could see no good coming of it.

Dad developed a notable distention of his abdominal area, and the doctor was not sure of the cause. The doctor ordered a CT scan to determine the cause of the distention. The facility did not have the equipment to conduct the CT scan, so an ambulance arrived at 8:00 PM to transport dad to the hospital. The staff at the facility told my mom and me that we could go to the hospital and wait for the ambulance. The emergency room was very busy for a Tuesday evening, and we did not know how long it was going to take them to complete the CT scan. Dad was acting very anxious and kept waving his right arm and reaching for the ventilator tube as if he were trying to remove it.

Three hours passed. It was after midnight, and we were still waiting for the CT scan. My mom noticed that my dad's blood pressure was dropping and mentioned it to the nurse. The ER doctor gave Dad something to raise his blood pressure, but it did not work.

Another hour passed, but dad did not respond to any attempts to increase his blood pressure. It continued to drop, and his heart rate dropped. Mom sat in a chair to the left of my dad and held his hand as the medical staff was tending to him. I was standing alongside my mom watching the scene unfold. At 1:10 AM, dad's heart stopped beating. The doctor injected his heart with a drug that should have started the heart again, but it did not. When the staff brought in a defibrillator we stopped them from making any further attempts to resuscitate him. When he passed away his eyes remained open halfway. The doctor reached up and closed his eyes. We came for a simple CT scan but instead Dad passed away. I realized the dream about Dad had come to fruition right before my eyes even though it felt like I was living a bad dream.

The doctor told us that he was sorry for our loss, and Mom and I went to a quiet room near the ER where we could sit down and gather ourselves. Neither of us had much to say as we were numb from the scene we had just witnessed. I knew if I began to cry that I probably would not be able to stop. After spending several minutes in the room, we decided to go home. I hoped I could make the drive home without any mishaps.

I dropped my mom off at her house and went on home. I pulled into the driveway and parked my truck. As soon as I turned the engine off, I immediately broke down and began sobbing uncontrollably. I remained in the truck for several minutes. When I went into the house, Gladys approached me in the kitchen. When she asked how my dad was doing, I told her that he had passed away about an hour earlier. My emotions were a mess, and I did not feel like talking. I was attempting to process the fact that my dad had passed away.

I walked over to my mom's house because I did not want her to be alone. We sat in her living room, but we did not talk. I spent that night on the sofa, dozing for short periods.

I was expecting Dad not to survive because of the dream. But when he passed away, it was difficult for me to process the loss. The many days of going to the hospital ended in such an unexpected manner. What we were living for weeks was now over. It was going to take time to work though the emotions of it all.

I had experience in planning funeral services, but never one that involved a close family member. My dad had arranged for his immediate burial, and that took place within a week after his passing. Mom made most of the memorial service plans with the pastor of her church. Ken, a friend and former co-worker of mine, put together a video to celebrate Dad's life.

The church was filled to capacity the day of the memorial service. Ken's video was exceptional and presented a pictorial history of my dad's life. During the service, people had the opportunity to share comments about my dad. To my surprise, my mom stood to say something. She said my dad used to say that they only had one fight: It started on their wedding day and lasted the entire time they were married. People did not expect that from my mom and everyone laughed.

The military funeral service for my dad occurred in mid-October. We waited for the cooler days of fall since the entire service was outdoors. This service gave those who could not attend the memorial service an opportunity to pay their respects. We experienced a warmer than normal fall, and the temperature that day was 102 degrees. Fortunately, these services take place in a covered Ramada.

This service had an element of finality. There were no further arrangements or memorial plans needed. There was a deep sense of "what now?" How does one move forward after such a loss? How do you recover from the loss of a person who was a husband, father, grandfather, and great-grandfather? My mom had been married to this man for over half a century, and now she faced living alone without him. There were many unanswered questions. If there was a pony in this pile, it was going to take time to find it.

To Think About:

1. Has someone close to you betrayed you or let you down? How did that make you feel? How did you react?

2. When have you betrayed someone or let someone down? Did you do anything to correct the situation?

3. Have you experienced the loss of someone close to you? How were you able to cope with the loss?

4. Do you think there is anything that can prepare you for the loss of a loved one?

5 – A Time to Heal

...a time to kill and a time to heal...

Ecclesiastes 3:3

I was not sure how I would respond when my dad passed away. It took a long time for me to realize why I felt the way I did about my dad. We engaged in many activities together when I was growing up and continuing in adulthood. He taught me how to work on cars, hunt and fish, and operate machinery.

Yet, despite all that, we never really had an emotional connection. I never heard the words "I love you" from my dad. To the best of my knowledge, he never heard those words from his father. Although he was a good provider for our family, he never gave us the emotional support we needed.

One of my seminary professors made a profound statement once in a class. He remarked that there are times we do not enter a relationship with some people until they are gone. This statement seemed impossible to understand at the time. How can a person enter a relationship with someone who is not physically present? The professor's comment made more sense after my dad passed away. I began to reflect upon the relationship my dad had with his father and what I had observed. I remembered there was no emotional bond between them. Their interactions mirrored the relationship my dad and I had. Though I think my dad and I had an underlying love for one another, we did not express it outwardly.

I began to understand that he could not give me something he did not possess - the ability to connect emotionally. Aside from being a good provider and teaching me how to accomplish tasks, he was simply not equipped to show love. Discovering the foundations of my feelings for my dad gave me a starting point for forgiveness, reconciliation, and healing.

About a month after my dad passed away, Gladys said something that shocked me. She said, "When are you going to get over it?" Whenever she made remarks such as this I chose not to respond. After her own father died of cancer in 1982 it took years for her to "get over" his passing. It stunned me when she made this comment and other hurtful ones within weeks after my dad passed away. Why did she insist on doing that?

After the military memorial service for my dad, Thanksgiving and Christmas were only weeks away. My dad always did most of the cooking for the holidays. Now that he was gone, who was going to cook? I did not think my mom wanted to, so our annual tradition for the holidays gave way to a new form. We managed to get through this first Thanksgiving and Christmas in my dad's absence with most of the family simply surviving and wanting to get past the holidays. I cannot remember who cooked that year. That first holiday season without my dad gave me a new appreciation for those who do not enjoy the holidays.

My friend Craig, my brother, and I went on a hunting trip two weeks before Christmas. Craig and I hiked to a vantage point on a mountain. From there we could see for miles in several directions. Craig decided to hike farther up the mountain, but I stayed behind. I sat down on a rock and looked out over a big valley. I sat there pondering and trying to process my dad's no longer being with us. More than 40 years earlier, my dad and I hunted together in the mountains I saw in the distance. My mind was not on hunting but on the loss of my dad and dealing with his passing. I was attempting to process this but knew it was going to take time.

My brother and I never discussed our dad's death, even on the hunting trip. I am not sure why we never did. When we were growing up, our family never shared emotions and feelings. Perhaps that was the dynamic behind our inability to discuss our loss. I knew how I was feeling, but I did not know how my brother was feeling. Perhaps I was afraid of showing emotion openly in front of my brother.

I was not the only one in the family having a hard time dealing with Dad's death. Our two daughters were the closest of all his grandchildren.

They struggled dealing with the reality that their grandpa was now gone. In fact, they still have moments when they have trouble coping with his death.

My mom was having a difficult time dealing with Dad's absence. We needed to look for help in dealing with our grief and discovered an organization, GriefShare, that assists those in the grieving process. An area church was hosting a new session the following January. My mom and I signed up to attend because I knew she would not go alone.

Each session we attended included a video exploring an aspect of the grieving process followed by discussion time. In one of the videos, the speaker made a statement that resonated with me. When we experience any loss in life the question "why?" often arises. He said (my paraphrase), "If God was sitting across the table from you and told you the 'why,' that still would not take away the pain." We may never know the "why" behind the loss, but we still ask that painful question. The amount of time it takes to work through the pain is different for each person. What may last weeks for one person may last years for another.

Several years ago, I spoke to a woman about loss. She had not experienced the death of a parent or spouse. I told her the time it takes to recover differs for everyone. She told me she thought five years should be enough to get over their pain. The truth is: There is no time limit on grief, but holding onto grief can become unhealthy. Grief is a process of letting go. Hanging onto grief can be debilitating.

In 2 Samuel 12, King David was pleading with God for the life of his newborn son. He did not eat for seven days, and although he did all that was humanly possible to save the child, the baby died anyway. After David learned of the child's death, he got up and ate. The attendants did not understand his actions and asked him why he was acting that way. David explained to them that while the child was alive he prayed and fasted. After his child died, he could not bring him back. That may seem callous, but David was right: Once someone has died, he or she is not coming back. Coming to grips with this is a key part of the grieving process. It is a hard reality, yes, but one that needs to be grasped if we are to heal.

When a person experiences a loss such as the death of a loved one, a friend, a marriage, or a job, it is in the person's best interest not to try to go through it alone. Try to find a good support group to join.

A starting place may be at a local church or mission. Others have experienced similar losses and can help you get through the constant challenges. New relationships you make in that environment will assist in the recovery process.

My mother was apprehensive about going to the GriefShare sessions. But after she started, she formed a friendship with one of the other attendees, Margaret. Both their husbands passed away around the same time, and both were Navy veterans. They had much in common and began talking on the phone daily. These sorts of friendships are beneficial in the grieving and healing process.

I continued struggling through grief, however. I had never experienced anything like that before. My experiences after my grandparents' deaths were very different from what I was feeling in the wake of Dad's death. So many things were left undone between my dad and me. There was no possibility of ever forming that missing emotional bond. Discovering the "why" behind the distant relationship came too late. Could the missing part of our relationship be reconciled even though he was gone? I took counseling classes during my undergraduate and graduate work. I studied the stages of grief and thought I knew what to expect. I was the one who counseled others who suffered a loss, but now I was no longer the counselor but the one who now needed help.

A New Normal

In the GriefShare sessions, they told us that what had been normal previously was no longer normal. With my dad gone, what was common for us was no longer common. My mom no longer drove, and I became the one who took her shopping and to appointments. This was all part of creating our new routine.

A few months before my dad passed away, my parents' long-running disagreement over getting a dog had ended. My dad wanted a dog; my mom did not. Friends of my parents called and told them about a stray dog found in their neighborhood. Dad persisted and finally got his dog, a Corgi mix. Dad started calling him "Buddy," and the name stuck. This little bundle of brown fur became an important part of the family after Dad passed away. The dog that my mom insisted she did not want has become a close companion.

Creating a new "normal" takes time. I have lunch with my mom almost every day and take Buddy out for his daily walks. I spend an hour and a half with my mom every evening and take the dog out for his last walk of the day. When I am gone, my mom's friend Margaret from GriefShare stays with her. They walk the dog together. This routine has become part of our new normal.

Everyone who suffers a loss develops a new system. When the person who did certain tasks is gone, someone must either assume those responsibilities or let them drop. In our situation, I am the one who assumed the duties. We have worked out a new system after much trial and error.

While we were in the process of developing our new normal, Gladys resented my evenings with my mom. Gladys and I were together for two hours each evening before I went to my mom's house. Yet for those two hours, Gladys would either be working crossword puzzles or in the other room on the computer. She complained about how we never interacted. This confused me. Though she did not like it when I went to my mom's, Gladys and I did not engage each other when together at home. What if it had been her mother who was left all alone? I wondered. Would the issue be the same? I could not understand why she had such a problem with my taking care of my mom. Gladys made me feel guilty for helping her.

One day Gladys said to me, "You and your mom make a better couple than we do." It was as if she were jealous of my mom.

Trying to Grieve

Though the GriefShare classes brought me to a later stage in my grief, I still needed time to process the loss of my dad. The tension in our home created an atmosphere that made it difficult for me to grieve. The disharmony and dissension created conditions unfavorable for healing. The declining relationship with Gladys diverted my focus and attention from grieving. So my grief came to resemble a physical wound that was not bandaged properly. A wound cannot heal if it is not taken care of appropriately.

My chaplain ministry aided me in the healing process because it temporarily removed me from the stress of home life. God allowed me to help others even though I was hurting. We can minister to other people as "wounded healers" even if we are going through trials.

Ministering to others during this period helped me because the focus was not on "me." I was not trying to focus on others to avoid what I was going through, but helping others helped me avoid dwelling on what I was experiencing. I learned a deep life lesson – not to be judgmental because I do not know what someone else is going through. The experience taught me to be less critical and more understanding of people. My loss enhanced my compassion towards those who have experienced similar losses. As it is with any experience, if we have not been through it ourselves we cannot totally understand it.

After my dad passed away, I was speaking with one of the women at the police department whose father had passed away two years earlier. I said to her, "If I had told you I knew what you are going through when your father passed away, I would have been lying." I had no idea what she was going through until I experienced it myself. Through the schooling of pain, the Master Teacher, God, is equipping us for His plan and purpose.

Wading through the manure of loss, these were valuable lessons that pointed to the pony in my pile.

To Think About:

1. Is there a relationship that you should work to improve or repair before the opportunity in this life is gone forever?

2. Where do you seek help if you are having a hard time coping with loss?

3. How can you help others in dealing with loss?

Note: Although I have no affiliation whatsoever with GriefShare, I would recommend attending a GriefShare program at a local church near you if you have lost a close family member. To find a local church in your area that is hosting a GriefShare support group, visit Church Initiative's web site at https://www.churchinitiative.org/.

6 – The Ordination Process

"For I know the plans I have for you," declares the LORD,
"plans to prosper you and not to harm you, plans to give
you hope and a future."

Jeremiah 29:11

I delivered my first sermon in September of 2000, during the weekend of the annual statewide denominational church camp. Most people from my church attended the camp, including Pastor Jake, so I arranged to fill in for him on Sunday in Phoenix. Since I was also attending camp, I rose early Sunday morning and left by 7:00 AM to arrive at the church in Phoenix on time.

Sunday began as a beautiful day. It was a cool and peaceful September morning and I could see the tall pines touching the blue sky. I tried to be quiet as I was leaving since many people were still asleep. Then, suddenly, the sound of my car alarm echoed throughout the camp. Somehow I had pressed the panic button on the car remote. I scrambled frantically trying to shut the alarm off. I am not sure how many campers the alarm woke up, but all I wanted to do was leave before they had a chance to form a mob.

I reached the church and people began arriving for the service. The music finished, and it was time for me to speak. Sermon notes in hand, I nervously made my way to the pulpit, hoping I could make sense of the notes. My sermon topic was on believers' need to pray and read our Bibles daily. It took not quite 15 minutes to exhaust my sermon notes. In my mind, those notes should have lasted *at least* 30 minutes. There

I was, standing in front of 50 people thinking to myself, "Now what?" I asked if anyone would like to come forward to the altar and pray. That was the only thing I could think to do. Seven people came forward, an illustration of what *God* can do. I am sure my dynamic sermon was not what led them to the altar. You see, God took what I thought was a fiasco and turned it into something positive.

I had begun the ordination process for the denomination two years before I became a chaplain. When I learned that most police chaplain positions require licensing or ordination I was more determined to pursue ordination.

Over the next two years, I completed the initial level of ordination requirements, including college courses and denominational requirements. I also preached, taught Sunday school, and visited the sick in local hospitals as part of the ordination process.

In the spring of 2002, our church began to plan for a new church building. Construction did not start until the needed funds became available. Many of us who attended the church spent months donating our labor to cut down on the construction costs.

One day when I was working at the church with Jake, he said, "You know what I like? *Loyalty.*" This statement took me aback, and I just looked at him for a moment. Then I ignored his comment and continued with what I was doing. Apparently, Jake wanted me to join those who mindlessly followed (i.e., were loyal to) him. I had witnessed what happened to people who did not follow his agenda. The "loyalty" worked in only one direction. He wanted loyalty but was unwilling to give it.

Staying on Course

It is difficult to convey the intensity of the ordination process. Education and preaching are only the most visible requirements. A pastor learns how to serve communion and perform infant dedications, adult baptisms, weddings, and funerals. More importantly, pastors must have a heart for people. No amount of education can take the place of loving the people you serve as a pastor.

I received scant guidance or instruction on the ordination process from anyone in my church. After I completed each phase in the process,

I needed to know what to do next but had no local assistance. There were times I felt I was fumbling about on my own. I made frequent calls to the national denominational headquarters for clarification of my next steps.

By September 2010, I finished my last class after more than 10 years of effort. I finally met the educational requirements for ordination. Or at least I *thought* I met all the requirements.

I attended the pastors' Christmas party that year at Jake's church. He and I were the last two people to leave. When he asked me if I was still taking my mother to church, I told him that I was. Mom attended a church in another denomination and no longer drove. I then asked, "Is there anything else I need to do before my ordination at the next annual church meeting in May?" He said, "No, nothing that I know of."

Meanwhile, I contacted the denominational headquarters to ensure all the paperwork was in place for my ordination. That December, I called the headquarters again. They told me that I had satisfied all the educational requirements for ordination and my local church would determine what further steps I needed to take.

Two months later, I received an email from headquarters.

> Dear Rick,
> We are currently working to prepare ordination status reports for each conference. Your annual conference office is the best resource for you regarding your ordination status.
>
> Kind Regards,
> <Person from Headquarters>

I had not heard anything from the local church. On April 6, 2011, I called the office and spoke with Lucy, the church secretary. I wanted to make sure I was approved for ordination at the upcoming meeting in May. Lucy told me that I was not on the agenda but assured me she would take care of it.

On April 9, I received a phone call from Harry, a member of the local church board and one of the two (horse)men with Jake the night they "pulled the plug" on our church plant. Harry advised me that the local board wanted me to attend a meeting a few days later.

At the meeting, Jake was there along with six board members. Jake asked me to tell the board what I had done to prepare for ordination. I gave a condensed version and told them that I had met all the educational and other requirements. After I finished, Jake said it was nice that I had completed all the work. The way he spoke revealed that he was leading up to something. I sat there anticipating hearing him say the word "but." Sure enough, he said, "But" and proceeded to say there was a concern since I was not regularly attending one of the denomination's churches. I felt my blood pressure rising. He knew that I took my mom to her church on Sunday because she had no other means of attending. I had discussed the issue with him at the Christmas party four months prior when he asked.

I explained to the board the situation with my mom, a widow who had no other means of getting to church. I maintained my composure throughout this ordeal. I was seething by the time the meeting was over because Jake had not only set me up but lied straight to my face. He had told me at the Christmas party that I did not need to do anything else toward ordination. Now, he was telling me it was a "concern" that I was not attending one of the denomination's churches regularly. This was confirmation that Jake lacked any hint of integrity. The unanswered question was, "Why did he do that?"

The annual meeting was one month away, and my ordination could not take place at that meeting as I had anticipated. A decade of working towards the goal was now potentially lost. This is what I would call *terminal disappointment*. A dishonest leader in the church was blocking the road to ordination. I had met all the criteria, yet for reasons unknown Jake was undermining me. If I had done something wrong, I could understand not receiving approval. Knowing I had done nothing wrong made it difficult to understand why Jake lied to me. I was at a loss.

I spent the weeks leading up to the annual meeting attempting to breathe some life back into my ordination. I called Harry to see what the committee had decided about my status. Harry told me that they had approved me. Jake was going to contact his superior for the final decision. His superior would be the one to determine if my ordination would take place. After my earlier experience, I was holding out little hope for approval. Jake had it out for me and had deceived me. There was no reason he would not lie to his superior about me to prevent him from endorsing me.

That same day, however, Jake was relieved of his position as the overseer of the Arizona churches. I could only speculate as to why Jake's superior decided to replace him. It was possible, I thought, that Jake's antics were catching up with him.

I knew that my ordination would not take place the following month. I struggled to make sense of what I was experiencing. This should have been a time of celebration, not one of confusion and searching for answers. "Why was this happening?"

The more I searched for answers, the more confused I became. When I had contacted the local church, they told me I needed to do one thing. When I had contacted headquarters, they told me I needed to do another. I began to question whether anyone knew what he or she was doing.

I contacted Jake's superior in hopes of finding something conclusive in my quest for answers. He did answer some of my questions and told me that due to the timetable involved my ordination could not take place the following month. He said he wished to meet with me and scheduled a meeting the afternoon before the annual meeting.

Two days before the annual meeting I called Lucy at the church office and asked her for copies of the minutes from the church meeting I had attended the previous month. She said she would try to email them to me after getting approval from Jake. Later, she told me that I could only have the portion of the minutes from the time I was at the meeting, meaning I could not know what took place after I left the meeting. As it turned out, I never received a copy of any minutes from Lucy.

Something was telling me not to go to the meeting with Jake's superior and Jake's replacement, but I went anyway. We met in Jake's office at the church. As soon as our meeting began, I sensed something was wrong. I thought they had already tried and convicted me before the meeting started. I was thinking to myself: "I wonder what Jake has told them about me?" Since Jake had lied before, I assumed he had lied to them about me.

The meeting lasted for an hour. Jake's superior did most of the talking. Jake's replacement (the overseer of the denomination's churches in Arizona) sat working on an electronic notepad during most of the meeting and seemed very disinterested. Jake's superior told me ordination was not necessary for my type of ministry. That was not true because many police departments require credentialing. He also mentioned that I was not attending one of their denominational churches regularly. I knew then that Jake had spoken to his superior about me sometime prior to the meeting, repeating the same sham criticism from a month earlier. This meeting was a complete waste because it accomplished nothing. After it was over, I realized that I should have skipped it altogether.

That evening the annual meeting took place. Though I stayed for the meeting, after what I had experienced in the meeting with Jake's superior earlier that day, I had no desire to be there. I had been part of this denomination for nearly 24 years, had done an enormous amount of work to get to this point, and it was as if nothing I had done counted for anything.

While sleeping that night, a voice came to me like a tidal wave in the middle of the night. I sat straight up in bed, heart racing. The voice said, "Don't let them do this to you. *Fight!*" So fight I did in the weeks that followed.

I emailed a letter to Jake's superior recapping what I was told about my ordination process, what Jake did in the meeting, and the situation after my father passed away. This email sparked off a salvo of emails. Nevertheless, the back-and-forth emails were an act of futility. My efforts to breathe some kind of life back into the ordination made no difference. I stated my case, but Jake's word took precedence over mine. I decided to stop the "fight" and ceased further contact with Jake's superior.

Several years prior to this, I told another pastor that "Christians shoot their wounded." He disagreed with me. From my vantage point, however, Christians do shoot their wounded. Though I had tried to do what was right by taking care of my mom, I suffered a penalty for doing so. When I should have received compassion and understanding from the leadership in the church, I received just the opposite.

Now What?

Up until the annual church conference in 2012, the denomination allotted me a certain amount of money each year for some of my chaplain expenses. I would save my receipts and mail them to Lucy at the church office for reimbursement, and she would mail me my reimbursement checks.

Lucy stopped sending my reimbursement checks when requested. It took weeks to get checks that were normally sent out within days. On one occasion, I drove to her office to pick up one of my checks. She made excuses and told me that she had already sent it to me. She blamed it on the postal service. The issue was not with the post office; it was with Lucy. She worked directly for Jake. My trust in her was declining rapidly, just like my trust in Jake.

I was trying to piece together some kind of reason why Jake and Lucy would do what they were doing. I had no rational answer to the question "Why?" There was a blank to fill in, and I was not sure what was going to fill it.

To Think About:

1. How do you handle a situation when no one will listen to you, yet you know truth is on your side?
2. "Should I stay or should I go" is the title of a popular song by The Clash. How does the title apply to situations in your life?
3. Have you been wounded by the church? If so, how did you respond? Could you overcome the sense of loss?

7 – The Departure

The one who calls you is faithful, and he will do it.
1 Thessalonians 5:24

My relationship with Gladys was in decline. We coexisted, living under the same roof, but as *married singles*. We were roommates living two separate lives. The chasm in the relationship was unbridgeable, as there was little communication or interaction between us.

Her behavior changed. She started buying more food than the two of us could ever eat. She increased her spending beyond our income with ever-increasing credit card balances and checking account overdrafts.

Gladys wanted me to get a job even though our income was sufficient, or so I had thought. I did not understand why I needed a job. If I had a job, my mom would lose her primary caregiver. Who would drive her to the doctor or take her shopping?

Months later, I realized why she wanted me to get a job. Her uncontrolled spending had more than doubled our debt beyond the level I knew about. She figured my extra income would cover the payments so I would never know about the extra debt.

Our discussions frequently turned into arguments, so I decided not to expend energy on them. Most conversations turned from discussing the issues to Gladys' questioning my character. Thus, we never resolved any of our real issues. After an argument, I usually initiated apologies to restore peace to the household. I am not claiming innocence, but this was not healthy. Finally, I said to myself, "I am not doing this any longer."

I printed monthly calendars and posted them on the refrigerator so we would know our upcoming schedules. I added our anniversary to the calendar when it came close. One day I looked at the calendar and realized Gladys had blotted out the word "anniversary" with white correction fluid. This left no doubt about her feelings concerning our marriage.

Our communication continued to decrease over time. About all we did together was go to church. We talked very little, which made the long ride seem even longer. During the week, Gladys would come home from work, do crossword puzzles or work on the computer with no interaction between us.

Meanwhile I continued my routine of chaplaincy and helping my mom. More than two years had passed since I had the dream about Gladys, and our coexistence was a miserable experience. All I kept thinking about and holding onto was God's telling me that He would take care of it.

Merry Christmas

On Christmas Eve morning 2011, I signed into one of my social media accounts. The first image I saw was of three dancing elves. My dad's face was on the middle elf and my daughters' were on each side. I felt myself getting angry. I sat at the computer and tried to ride out the anger. This was the second Christmas since my dad had passed away, and his absence remained fresh in the family members' memories. When I saw my dad's face pasted on an animated dancing elf, I thought "enough is enough!"

My attempt to avoid anger failed. I knew Gladys had posted the images. I rose from the chair and confronted her in the kitchen. I told her to remove the images from the computer. Then I put my jacket on and went outside to regain my composure. I found out later that my daughters had seen the dancing elves and seeing their grandfather's face upset them to tears, particularly at Christmas.

After I calmed down I went back in the house and sat in the living room. I heard Gladys loading her car. I thought she was packing items for a pre-Christmas meal with family at our oldest daughter's house. As she went toward the car, I asked, "Are you leaving?" She replied, "Have a nice life." Then she walked out the door.

My mom and I went to the family get-together that afternoon. Gladys was there, but she would not talk to me or even acknowledge my presence. It was clear then that she had not just loaded items to take to the party; she was loading her clothes and belongings so she could move in with our daughter.

On Christmas Day, I awoke to an empty house – no wife, no kids, just me, alone for the first time on Christmas. When I called her a week later, Gladys told me we could get a legal separation. She planned everything that we were going to do. I was thinking of what God had planned, not what she had planned.

When we met for lunch three weeks later, Gladys informed me that she had gone to see a counselor and told the counselor that she did not want to be married anymore.

Items began vanishing from the house. She knew my routine, of course, and avoided me. We had photographs of our families attached to cabinet doors in the kitchen. Gladys removed and destroyed all my family's photographs, including those of nieces and nephews who had done nothing to her.

Given our poor financial condition and high debt, we knew bankruptcy was inevitable. I made the mistake of trusting her. She continued to charge high-dollar purchases, and the reason she wanted me to get a job became ever clearer. She did not want to control her spending.

Charge It!

I developed a pain in my mid-lower abdomen brought on by the stress with Gladys and constant calls from creditors. To get some relief, I eliminated all non-essential expenses.

Gladys emailed me a list of items she wanted, and I placed them together in the garage. She and our daughter came to pick up the items. She told our daughter, "Except for the wedding photos, probably just burn those." We loaded her vehicle and the two left. This was the last time Gladys came to the house. After hearing Gladys' comment I hid all our wedding photographs.

In mid-April, I met over coffee with one of the officers from the police department. She needed to talk about some of the challenges in her life. I felt impressed to speak to her about her spiritual life during the conversation. The time came for us to talk about Jesus. When I asked her if anyone had ever explained salvation to her, she said, "No." I told her God sent His son, Jesus, to earth to be a sacrifice for our sins. We all sin, which is why we need a savior in the person of Jesus. He died on a cross for us, lay in a tomb for three days, and rose from the dead. Our hope is in the person of Jesus and the empty tomb, but we need to invite Him into our life.

After I finished, she said, "Let's do it." We were sitting at a table outside and she did not want to pray at the table. So we walked to her parked car, and I led her in a prayer to accept Jesus into her life. Remarkably, the only people who knew what I was going through were my family and the police chief. God does not stop working because of what we are experiencing personally. He works despite what we are experiencing.

Moving On

Gladys and I prepared the paperwork for the bankruptcy attorney. When I called the attorney's office the following week, they told me that I qualified for bankruptcy but Gladys did not. After speaking with the bankruptcy attorney and finding out how much Gladys tried to hide in the bankruptcy documentation, I called a divorce attorney and made an appointment.

Meanwhile, my brother and I went on a hunting trip. I needed time to process everything and seek what the Lord wanted me to do. This was 38 years of marriage at stake. One night I woke up about midnight. I prayed for several hours asking the Lord what I needed to do about divorcing Gladys, and did not go back to sleep. The Lord told me to divorce her, confirming what I had heard in my dreams years earlier. I had peace about what I had to do.

I met with the divorce attorney in early May. Going to that office was one of the hardest things I have ever done. Divorce was something that happened to *other people* and was contrary to everything I believe.

Church Meeting Time Again

The week after I met with the divorce attorney, I attended the annual regional church meeting in Phoenix. A month before, Jake had sent me a letter expressing his regret over what he had done to me in regards to my ordination.

Jake was also at the annual meeting, so I had an opportunity to speak to him face-to-face. I told him it was nice that he was sorry for what he had done and then asked him, "What are you going to do to fix it?" He told me that his superiors were watching him closely. When he said that, I knew he was not going to do anything about my ordination. It did not matter anymore because I was entering the divorce process and facing an uncertain future.

I was trying not to let the circumstances dictate how I was acting or feeling. This was the worst and most stressful time of my life. I would have rather faced a bus full of armed robbers than face what was coming. I was not sure I was going to have a place to live or a vehicle to drive when this was over. I could not process any emotion of loss because preparing for bankruptcy and divorce filings occupied all my time.

In mid-May, the attorney filed the divorce papers with the court. In the latter part of the month, I received a text message from Gladys: "So are you filing for bankruptcy by yourself then?" I replied, "Yes. I will get with you later." She responded, "Great communication." She had not received the divorce papers by then, and I knew she would cease all communications with me once she saw them.

Meanwhile one of my favorite pet dogs was euthanized. She had lived in our house when my daughters were growing up and later moved with my youngest daughter and her husband. With all the other things going on, the dog's death added more stress. My son-in-law and I buried the dog. I remember that day saying to myself, "I do not know how much more I can take."

The problems of June continued the entire month. One of my hips began to hurt so severely that I could barely walk. A baseball-sized spot appeared for no apparent reason on the calf of my right leg and began to turn purple like a bruise. I did not go to the doctor for any of these ailments. I determined that God would take care of my physical problems or I would live with them.

In early July, I found a bankruptcy attorney because legally I could not use the same one Gladys and I had seen together. During the appointment, we reviewed the debt and I explained my situation. He confirmed that bankruptcy was my best course of action. I was not aware of all the debts Gladys had incurred. She continued to use credit cards in both our names, and letting the financial situation continue to fester could lead to higher liability for unpaid bills.

The phone calls from bill collectors ceased after I met with the attorney. My stress level dropped, but I still dealt with the fallout from the divorce filing. I could not file bankruptcy before the divorce was final without disrupting both legal proceedings.

Meanwhile, the spouse of a city official passed away, and the official asked me to conduct the memorial service. If feelings guided me, I would not have done it. I did not want to add that load to all that was happening in my life. I led the service anyway, and it was the right thing to do. Two hundred people attended.

I received a phone call from one of the police officers in mid-July. A car ran over and killed a five-year-old boy, and some of the responders were having a tough time dealing with the aftermath. Responding to calls like this is never easy, especially since some of the officers had children the same age as the little boy. The thing that bothered me most when I was an officer was dead children. I made sure the officers were doing as well as they could afterward. Everyone processes these incidents differently. Some officers tend to internalize their feelings, which is an unhealthy way to cope with the emotions.

But Wait, There's More...

Not surprisingly, by August Gladys stopped communicating with me. A collection agency contacted me later that month about one of Gladys' business credit cards. When I told the woman that Gladys did not live here anymore, she said, "That's okay. I can talk to you since you are listed on the card also." I said, "What?" Gladys used my name without my knowledge and she used the name of the church plant without authorization. I added, "That's fraud." Gladys applied for the credit card a month after the church ceased meeting. When I told my divorce attorney, she commented, "You don't even know who you are married to anymore, do you?" All I could say was, "No, I don't."

Several months later, Gladys and I appeared in divorce court with our attorneys. Up until the hour of the proceedings, my attorney and I encountered obstacles, lack of responsiveness, and delaying tactics. As it turned out, we were in the courtroom less than 10 minutes and it was all over. Almost four decades of marriage ended. The revelation I received in a series of dreams almost four years earlier had now happened.

This was not what I would call a victorious day for me. I felt more pain and loss. Knowing that I was doing what God told me to do did not diminish the heartache.

I could not take time to grieve and process the end of a marriage because I had to start on the bankruptcy proceeding. I had more questions than answers, a completely unsettling experience. I prepared a mountain of paperwork for the divorce and I needed to generate another mountain for the bankruptcy. God had not mentioned this part to me. I knew the divorce was coming but not the bankruptcy.

To Think About:

1. Have you personally been impacted by divorce? How has it affected you?

2. In what circumstances do you think divorce is acceptable?

3. If you are married, what parts of life do you and your spouse not share? Are there potential problems in those unshared areas?

8 – The Bankruptcy

*And we know that in all things God works for the good
of those who love him, who have been called according to
his purpose.*

Romans 8:28

The divorce final, it was time to proceed with the bankruptcy. I
met with the bankruptcy attorney the day after the divorce was
final. We needed to submit the paperwork to the federal court
as soon as possible. Though I did not want to file, there were no other
alternatives. I did not know if other debts might be lurking around
because Gladys had already used my name without my knowledge to
obtain a credit card.

In mid-March, as the time for filing the case was drawing near, I
met with the paralegal at the attorney's office. We reviewed the final
papers for completeness and verified that we were ready to file. As I
drove out of the parking lot, an inaudible voice said, "You pass." I believe
the Lord was saying I "passed" because I had revealed everything in the
bankruptcy and did not try to hide anything.

The attorney filed my case in federal court in late March 2013.
When the court receives a bankruptcy case, a trustee takes over the
case. The trustee reviews the paperwork and then requests any further
information needed to complete his investigation. I responded to the
trustee's request, and a court date was set.

In early May, I appeared in federal bankruptcy court in downtown
Phoenix. My attorney briefed me before I appeared before the trustee.

I was the fourth person called. The trustee swore me in and asked me a series of questions. We were done in five minutes.

The hearing was over, but I was not finished. I had to appear in federal court again to see if I could keep my vehicle. I had considered selling my truck several months earlier. One night I woke up to an inaudible voice telling me to "keep the truck." This was my sign not to sell my vehicle.

More Loss

My youngest daughter was about two months pregnant with her second child. In mid-May, she sent me a text message asking me to pray because she felt like she was losing the baby. After reading her message, I sat down on the sofa and cried. The following day she went to her obstetrician who confirmed that the baby was dead.

The loss of this baby was devastating. My daughter had difficulty bearing children, and I wondered if she might not want to try again or might not be able to carry another baby. Times such as this bring many questions, the biggest of which is "Why?" I remember what the person said in our grief class, though, that even if we knew "why" it would not remove the pain.

On Memorial Day, my youngest daughter sent me pictures of my dad's grave marker. His birthday came one day before Memorial Day. I think she was dealing with the loss of her grandfather and the loss of her unborn child.

In mid-June I was back in bankruptcy court. The judge asked me a few questions, but my attorney did most of the speaking. When we were finished, the judge said, "You keep the truck." The whole process lasted five minutes. The voice that came to me in the middle of the night months before knew well in advance that I was going to keep my truck.

More Bad News

In mid-summer 2013, we received news that my niece Julie's husband, Brad, had developed a pre-leukemia condition. His condition was serious but treatable. Although his future was uncertain, he remained in good spirits and maintained an optimistic outlook. He did not improve, however, even after multiple hospital admissions. His condition deteriorated from pre-leukemia to full leukemia.

During one of Brad's stays in the hospital, he developed a rash over his entire body. He was under heavy sedation, but at times he would sit up in bed, speak, and then lie down. One night he yelled out "Hebrews 4" and then immediately lay down. I asked my niece if he was reading the Bible I gave him. She said she did not think so. We could not figure out why he said Hebrews 4. I think God was working in him despite the illness and his mental condition.

In mid-August I received notice from the trustee that my bankruptcy was "discharged," relieving me of all debt, including the debt I knew about and any debt that I was not aware I had. The case was finished, but it was, like the day the divorce was final, a bittersweet day. I was glad that the case was over but not happy about being in that situation.

The following month I contacted the court about the conduct of Gladys' divorce attorney. Her attorney had failed to respond to most of my attorney's correspondence and submitted incorrect papers to the court. These actions cost time and thousands of dollars in extra fees. I decided it was time to do something about it.

I later learned that others had filed similar complaints about the attorney. The court ruled that the allegations were justified, which resulted in the loss of her law license and a substantial fine.

Brad went back into the hospital in early October. The doctors were now looking for a bone marrow donor because a marrow transplant was one of the final efforts in fighting the leukemia.

On October 12, I performed a wedding ceremony. That date is special for our family because it was my parents' wedding anniversary. The groom-to-be was the son of one of the retired sergeants I know from the Phoenix Police Department. The wedding took place in a public park and the weather cooperated. This was the first time I signed a wedding license on the hood of a pickup truck. There is a redneck joke in there somewhere.

Four days later, I became very ill. My throat was hurting so bad I could hardly swallow. I went to the doctor who prescribed large doses of antibiotics. The following week, I began to develop white spots in my throat. I woke up one night shaking uncontrollably. I could not remember ever being this ill. I made another appointment with the doctor who told me to finish the antibiotic.

A day later, those white spots in my throat turned into a solid white mass. It was the weekend, and I did not want to wait for the following week to return to the doctor. I went to a clinic and received a prescription for medication to combat the condition in my throat. By the middle of November, my throat had not cleared up. I returned to the clinic and was prescribed another medication to help rid my throat of the white spots.

We celebrated Thanksgiving at my mom's house the Sunday before Thanksgiving. That year we took the easy way out and ordered pizza and wings. That was our non-traditional Thanksgiving meal. On Thanksgiving Day, I went to Brad and Julie's house. The doctors allowed Brad to go home for Thanksgiving. He had undergone chemotherapy treatments and lost all his hair.

I visited Brad in the hospital on December 12. The search for a marrow donor was successful. The doctors wanted the leukemia to be in remission before performing the marrow transplant. We were not sure how things were going to turn out for Brad because his condition was not improving. I wanted to make sure he was right spiritually in the event he did not survive the illness. He and I were alone in his room, a rare opportunity for me to speak to him without any interruptions. After a few minutes of conversation, I asked him if he would like to pray and ask Jesus into his life. He said, "Yes." We prayed together and he accepted Jesus into his life. No matter the outcome, Brad was ready.

Three days before Christmas, a friend and I went to see Brad at the hospital. My niece was there. We brought him a little remote-controlled helicopter that fires plastic projectiles, and he sure perked up when he saw it. I told him he could chase nurses with it. We had a good visit and prayed with him.

Christmas Day was uneventful for my mom and me. Two years had passed since Gladys walked out. A neighbor came over to my mom's house, and we had biscuits and gravy for breakfast.

Four days after Christmas, the family came to my mom's house for another non-traditional family Christmas meal. We decided to go with the same meal we had for Thanksgiving – pizza and wings. The kids like it and clean-up is easy. The main thing is that we could have family time.

The police chief approached me about delivering the invocation for the dedication of the new police station scheduled for late January. I told him I would do it. Many local officials would attend the dedication. This included officers from the nearby military base.

The day of the dedication was a flurry of activity. Crews set up chairs under a large canopy. The fire department bagpipe band played to start the service. I estimate that 200 people attended. After the city manager spoke, I took the podium to offer the prayer of dedication.

That evening, I went to a meeting of fellow police chaplains. Near the end of the meeting I received a text message informing me that two of our officers were involved in a shooting. I left the meeting and drove directly to the scene of the shooting. The officers were unharmed but noticeably shaken. I spoke with them and attempted to ease their stress. Considering what they had just experienced, both were doing well.

A week later, the officers went to the shooting range to qualify so they could return to normal duties. I went along to observe. Officers sometimes have difficulty firing a pistol after such an incident. The officers easily passed the qualification. I think I was as relieved as they were.

In early February, my mom called and said her dog Buddy had bitten her finger. I knew there had to be more to the story because he would not bite without reason. Once I began to probe how the dog "bit" my mom it made more sense. My mom was out walking the dog. He was eating something he picked up, and when she tried to take whatever it was out of his mouth, that is when she was "bitten." The one thing you do not want to do is get between that dog and a morsel of anything edible. My traumatized mom did recover.

In mid-February, I performed a wedding ceremony for an officer. I arrived early the day of the wedding. The family was scurrying about with last-minute preparations. We had no rehearsal, so this was going to be interesting. I had performed weddings like that before, and they make me nervous. I always think about what can go wrong. This wedding went well, however, and there were no major mishaps.

In early March, I met my youngest daughter for lunch. She was pregnant again. By this time, she was well past the two-month mark, the point at which she lost her baby the previous May. Three months later, she gave birth to a healthy baby boy, which I think helped ease the pain of the loss of her baby a year earlier.

In late March, I went to visit Brad at the hospital in Phoenix. He was not doing well. The leukemia was not responding to any of the treatments, and the marrow transplants were making no difference. It was difficult seeing this 31-year-old young man in that condition.

By early April, the doctors could do no more for Brad and transferred him to a hospice. Two days later my brother called and told me that Brad had passed away that morning with family members at his side. He told me that when Brad passed away he had a smile on his face and a tear came rolling down his cheek. I believe this was a bittersweet picture of the sadness of leaving loved ones behind and looking ahead to a life eternal.

My niece was making funeral arrangements. She called and asked if I would read Hebrews 4 at the service because Brad had blurted out "Hebrews 4" when he was in the hospital. I told her I would do it.

A large crowd of friends, family, and co-workers attended the service. Many stood in the doorway to observe the service. When my turn to speak came, I explained why we were reading Hebrews 4 and then read it to the crowd. After the church service, there was a short graveside service. I remember looking at my niece and her three young children. She was now a 31-year-old widow. The two younger children were not old enough to understand what had happened to their dad. I was trying to make sense of it all. There was that haunting question again: "Why?"

Two weeks after Brad's funeral, my mom became very ill and developed a fever. When she volunteered to go to the emergency room, I knew it was bad. An x-ray revealed she had pneumonia. With her lung condition, this was not good. They considered admitting her to the hospital. One of the considerations in not admitting her was the possibility of contracting an infection while in the hospital. That would just exacerbate her condition. We decided to take her home. She was very weak, and I would have to keep a close watch on her.

The following afternoon I took her to see the doctor. He prescribed medication, and she took it with no argument. When Mom did not argue with the doctor, I knew how sick she was. A routine had developed between my mom and her doctors. They would tell her what she needed to do, and if she did not agree with them, she would tell them she was not going to do it. The doctors got tired of arguing with her and started merely *suggesting* what she needed to do and left it at that.

It took several months for my mom to recover from the pneumonia. I was not sure if she was going to survive. She finally got better and settled back into her "routine" with the doctors.

Life's Surprises

Life confronts us with many unplanned situations. Bankruptcy was something I had not planned. My niece did not plan to lose her husband. My daughter did not plan to lose an unborn child. My mom did not plan to get sick. No matter what we may face when challenged, what counts is how we respond to it. Going through bankruptcy was a necessary but a humbling experience. It represented failure – failure that was public for all to see. That was the most difficult aspect of this for me. Most people were gracious and not condemning. I think I was probably my worst critic.

When we go through trials, we must dig below the surface and look for the hidden lesson and ask: What can I take away from the experience? My take-away from this was twofold. First, I learned the financial mistakes not to repeat. Second, I learned that I needed to remember to put things in perspective. The bankruptcy was a painful and an unwanted occurrence. But compared to the losses that my niece and daughter experienced, the bankruptcy was not so significant. I can recover from the monetary loss, but once life is lost, there is no hope of recovery.

We sometimes question where God is when we are going through trials. He is at our side, right where He always is. God may be silent, but He is there. I think the silence is a test to see how we are going to react to what we are experiencing. How we react is dependent upon our relationship with Him. When facing difficulties, our challenge is to learn to depend upon Him in bad times as well as good. This is not easy when we are surrounded by problems. If we are to have peace in the storms, however, there is no safer place than under the wing of our Creator.

To Think About:

1. Have you experienced the death of someone close to you? How did you process the loss?

2. How can you help someone who is experiencing this type of loss?

3. What keeps you going through dark times and the possible depression that may follow? Have you been tempted to or are you turning to drugs, alcohol, or other distractions to numb the pain? How do you think God fits into your pain?

9 – Forgiveness…Not an Option

Then Peter came to Jesus and asked, "Lord, how many times shall I forgive my brother or sister who sins against me? Up to seven times?" Jesus answered, "I tell you, not seven times, but seventy-seven times."

Matthew 18:21-22

Nothing had prepared me for the loss of my father, rejection by the church, my wife leaving, divorce, and bankruptcy. I attended counseling classes in college and received training in critical incident response for my police chaplain duties. When helping people deal with these situations in my counselor role, though, I was always on the "outside looking in." Now, I was on the "inside looking out." As with any of our circumstances in life, we cannot completely understand until we experience it personally. I knew God would get me through regardless of the circumstances. I had no idea *how* He would get me through but I had the confidence that He would get me through.

I faced so many uncertainties. I was not sure if I was going to lose my house or have enough money to pay bills after divorce and bankruptcy. The conflicts created a spiritual tug of war within me. Part of me questioned if there would be enough money to survive. The other part of me was trying to trust God for the necessary funds. I knew God had a plan, but my uncertainty about how I was going to survive produced many uncertainties.

I thought I had a large amount of faith, but now it was on trial. Not knowing what the future held was like looking down a long dark corridor and seeing no light. I had never faced anything like this before. The security I once knew was gone. The uncertainty of what was ahead made me uneasy. I knew God had not brought me to that moment to abandon me. *That* was the ray of light in that dark corridor.

I believe God takes us through these valleys to help us mature. While we are in the valley, we may not see what He is trying to accomplish. We can only see what He was doing when we have a chance to look back, maybe years later. These are times of spiritual conditioning. Just as someone doing physical weight training uses resistance to build muscle, so in spiritual training we grow through resistance. And many times we may feel the weight of the world is on us, but we learn to keep moving forward.

As we press through our circumstances, we develop spiritual "muscles." They cultivate trust in our Christian walk. God does not take us through the difficult periods of life for no reason. We may question God about "why" we are going through the garbage. Maybe we need to be asking "What?" rather than "Why?" What is God teaching me? Is He teaching me patience? Is He strengthening my faith? Am I learning to be more obedient? Look past the circumstances and find out what the lesson is.

One of the lessons God taught me became apparent not long after everything unraveled. I felt anger toward those who had wronged me. My obstacle of unforgiveness fueled my anger. It was not just a track-and-field hurdle but more like a six-foot brick wall complete with razor wire on top. Getting over this wall was hard.

God's Word is specific about forgiveness. There is no other option but to forgive. The Bible says nothing about this is easy, but it is necessary. By nature, we want to hang on to our anger and unforgiveness. We believe that we are entitled to embrace the feelings we experience when we are treated unfairly. Living in the anger and hurt is the easy way to stay the same. As long as we hang on to our anger we do not need to work at forgiveness. When God tells us to forgive, it is for us rather than for the person who wronged us. Forgiveness takes time and will not happen in an instant. I learned this the hard way, from my own experience. I think I am doing fine and then something triggers a thought and I am back in the anger again. I learned to pray and ask for help in these moments. Over time, this approach – praying for God's assistance – helped me get through the periods when I fell back into unforgiveness.

Changes

Changed relationships added to my feeling of loss, especially when friends found out I was divorced. Some people I had known for years became more distant. Some friends, however, remained faithful throughout the changes.

Those who have lost a spouse undergo similar changes in relationships. Married friends may see a person who is no longer "attached" differently and distance themselves. These changed relationships add to feelings of loneliness and rejection. At times it feels like a penalty for being single again.

My wife and I were friends with a couple for many years. They divorced several years ahead of us. Less than a month after my divorce was final, the divorced friend suggested that she wanted to begin a relationship. I told her I was not ready, and when she persisted I ceased contact with her. I needed time to heal, and she did not understand why I was not ready.

The wife of another friend passed away and I presided over her funeral service. About a week after the funeral, I asked my friend how he was coping with the loss of his wife. He told me women were asking him over to their homes for dinner, even at the cemetery after we finished the graveside service.

When he shared this with me, I wondered about the motivations behind such invitations. Maybe they were trying to be nice. He was at the beginning of his grieving process. Processing the loss of a spouse takes months or even years, and a person cannot grieve properly if he is trying to begin a new relationship.

Grieving is a time to heal. If healing has not taken place, the grief passes into the next relationship. Therefore, it is important to be well along in healing before moving into the next relationship. Someone who has recently divorced or lost a spouse should wait at least a year before attempting to form another relationship.

Whom Can You Trust?

It is difficult to express the pain I experienced through my series of "life events." Those I trusted most were the ones at the root of my pain. That is what upset me the most. I did not know whom to trust. I could not trust those in the church or my spouse.

I visited the optometrist for an eye exam. My glasses were several years old, and the prescription needed updating. When I picked up the glasses a week later, they seemed to be fine – until I drove at night. The reflections of the headlights off street signs made the signs look fuzzy. My old glasses did not have this problem. So I took the eyeglasses back and was assured they would correct the problem.

When I went back to pick up the corrected glasses two weeks later, the optometrist met me at the front counter and gave me the eyeglasses. He acted a bit odd when he handed me the eyeglasses and turned and walked away. Something was wrong with his body language.

I tried the glasses at night and discovered they had the same issue. I think he gave me back the same pair. I could not prove it, so I reverted to wearing my old glasses. The money I spent on these long-awaited eyeglasses was wasted. I could not even trust my eye doctor.

Sometimes I felt as if I were detached from the world and living in an emotional fogbank. Disconnected and just going through the motions is the best way I can describe it. I asked a psychology teacher about my sense of detachment. He told me that this was a normal reaction to high stress levels. It is the body's defense and coping mechanism. That relieved my fears because I thought I had an ailment.

My thinking became cynical and I trusted people less, much like my approach when I was a police officer. As an officer, I dealt with people who were not always trustworthy. I witnessed inconceivable crimes. My pastor for over 15 years betrayed me. My wife of 38 years betrayed me. I never imagined that my pastor or wife would hurt me so deeply.

What to do?

In the aftermath of the season of loss – of my father, my church, my wife, and my financial security – I had to decide how to proceed. I did not want to sit around and wallow in the manure pile. I chose to move on, but finding a starting point was difficult. No matter the starting point, I had to start somewhere to begin the healing process.

In seminary, we learned the three "H's": "Hurt," "Hate," and "Heal." The "hurt" is the initial stage when we experience a traumatic loss. The trauma leaves one feeling numb and in a state of disbelief similar to the shock people experience when they receive the traumatic news that they have a terminal illness or a loved one has died unexpectedly. There is an initial feeling of unbelief.

The "hate" stage is when we experience anger. Getting angry is all right when a person has experienced loss. We are equipped with the emotion of anger. We see in scripture that Jesus got angry but He did not let His anger become unhealthy (Matthew 12:12). When does anger become unhealthy? When anger rules the person, and the person does not rule the anger. In the Phoenix area, there have been numerous cases of "road rage" over the past several years. Some have resulted in drivers' deaths. These are extreme examples, but they illustrate what happens when the emotion rules the person to an unhealthy level. Get angry, but do not let your anger elevate to a level of unhealthiness (Ephesians 4:26). Just getting angry will accomplish nothing. What I have learned is the importance of channeling anger into something productive. This was yet another lesson I learned while going through these times.

During the divorce, Gladys' attorney made me angry with delay tactics and the associated additional costs. I could have remained angry and done nothing, building myself into a frenzy of bitterness, but instead I channeled the anger into something productive by filing a complaint against her attorney.

The last "H" is "heal." Once through the first two stages, true healing can take place. There is no timetable of how long it will take to get through the healing process. It is God's and your timetable, not anyone else's. People who try to push others through the healing process have obviously not been through the same experience.

When going through the healing process, there will be times when we will take a step backwards. The world is fine, all is well, and then something will trigger a thought, and suddenly the thoughts are back in the middle of the trauma. Maybe a thought brings up a feeling of anger towards a person. This is normal. Forgiveness does not mean forgetting. Forgiveness is working past the hurt and pain. It is working past the vengeful "I am going to make them pay" stage. It is about forgiving the person who has hurt you. Remember: Forgiveness is not about the other person; it is about you.

Unforgiveness or harboring ill feelings towards someone is only affecting YOU. The person you are mad at most likely is not even concerned about you. The only thing unforgiveness does is make you bitter. When bitterness takes root, it will affect you and those around you. Left unchecked, bitterness can and will affect your health. "Bitterness is like drinking poison and waiting for the other person to die."[1]

Forgiveness is not an option (Matthew 6:15, Luke 6:37). While nailed to a cross, Jesus said, "Father, forgive them, for they do not know what they are doing" (Luke 23:34). While he was stoned to death, Stephen said, "Lord, do not hold this sin against them" (Acts 7:60). What do our circumstances look like compared to these two examples? Most of our circumstances are nowhere near as dire. If Jesus and Stephen can ask God to forgive in these moments, who are we to harbor any unforgiveness towards anyone? If healing is to take place, we *must* forgive.

Not a Matter of Mathematics

The exchange about forgiveness between Jesus and Peter in Matthew 18 is not a matter of mathematics. When Peter asked Jesus how many times we are to forgive, Peter suggested up to seven times. Jesus said we are to forgive not seven times but seventy-seven times. The seventy-seven times would equal 490. It is not that we are to forgive 490 times and stop. What Jesus is saying is that we are not to stop forgiving – *ever*.

Do not expect to have peace in your life if you refuse to forgive. Peace is a product of the choice you make to forgive. I have never met anyone full of bitterness who is at peace with himself or those around them. Some of the people I have worked with are never happy. They allowed bitterness to take root and nothing ever makes them cheerful. They complain about almost everything and are very negative. I could hand them a shiny brick of pure gold and they would find something wrong with it. They will rob you of your peace and joy. Even worse, you can become this type of person if you do not forgive. When you are going through difficult times, these sorts of people do not need to be part of your life. Find those who will help and not hinder.

God extends His mercy and grace to us. "Mercy is God's withholding judgment or evil that I deserve; grace is God's giving me blessing or good

---

1. Joanna Weaver, Having a Mary Spirit: Allowing God to Change Us from the Inside Out (Colorado Springs, CO: WaterBrook Press, 2006), p. 153.

that I do not deserve."[2] I have defined grace and mercy as "something we want but have a difficult time giving." If you think about it, that is true. When someone offends us, we tend to want to get back at that person — to even the score. In our humanness, our first reaction is to think about hurting those who hurt us. We should do just the opposite. Before we react, we need to step back and ask ourselves how God wants us to handle the situation. Sometimes we will need to talk it out and repair the relationship. Sometimes we will need to let it go and move on. We cannot afford to leave God out of these times. Rather, we must seek God's wisdom in how to handle these situations.

What would it look like if God reacted to us in the manner we tend to react to others when we are offended? This is a scary thought, is it not? If God treated us as we treat people who have offended us, what would that be like? Our view of God would not be favorable. When we commit a sin, it is an offense against God, yet His reaction to us is not harsh or vindictive. If we are willing to acknowledge our offense, He is willing to forgive us. This is our example of how we are to respond to those who offend us. I know that some of us have suffered great harm at the hands of others. These are complicated circumstances, yet with time, forgiveness can take place. Remember, forgiveness is a process and does not occur instantaneously.

I questioned God: What do I do with all the memories of nearly 40 years of marriage? How could I fall out of love with someone? These are difficult questions to answer. When my wife left, I could not just turn off the emotions. All I heard God say was, "Turn them over to Me." Good or bad, we all have memories etched in our minds. How we deal with them is important. Dwelling on and living in the past is not good for us – especially when we are dwelling on past hurts. Hanging on to the past can be an obstacle to spiritual growth. We need to deal with past hurts and let them go. Give them a proper "burial" and move on. The Bible teaches us to put our hand to the plow and not look back (Luke 9:62).

Why does a car have a big windshield and a small rearview mirror? Because the driver spends most of his time moving forward and only occasionally glances in the rearview mirror. We can reflect on the good

---

2. David Reagan, http://www.learnthebible.org/what-is-grace.html.

times and not dwell on the bad. To heal we need to turn our past hurts over to God and reflect on the good times rather than dwell on the bad.

We need to follow Jesus' example of forgiveness. If we do not forgive, then we cannot expect God to forgive us (Matthew 6:15). God *must* be in the forgiveness equation. Our efforts alone cannot accomplish forgiveness. God is the One who gives us the power to forgive.

God's Word is clear: We must forgive. God requires it of us, and it is for our own good. Is it easy? No. It takes time and effort to forgive. Spiritual growth cannot take place if we harbor unforgiveness towards another. When true forgiveness occurs, we are set free from the bonds of unforgiveness.

Remember, forgiveness is not an option.

To Think About:

1. Have you dealt with loss? What did you do to cope with loss? Looking back, is there anything you would do differently in coping with loss?

2. Do you still need to forgive some people for long-ago hurts? What keeps you from doing so?

3. How do you respond to what the Bible teaches about forgiveness? What challenges you about these approaches?

10 – Why the Adversity?

Then Job took a piece of broken pottery and scraped himself with it as he sat among the ashes.

Job 2:8

I recovered slowly from all the events and losses: my dad passed, my church rejected me, my wife left, we got divorced, and I went bankrupt – all in a four-year period. I did not return to some sense of normalcy for two years after I lost my dad. Meanwhile, the promise of ordination slipped away after a decade of preparation. In the middle of everything else, my wife left. Then I ended up in a dire financial situation that led to bankruptcy. I could not recover from one situation before another arose. My physical health suffered from the stress of all that happened. I was an emotional mess.

I struggled to understand why I was going through these challenges. I always tried to do the right thing in my life and treated people fairly. I could not understand what I had done to deserve these troubles. I could understand my dad's passing because that was the natural order of things. But what had I done wrong for my life to be such a mess? Previously, my life had been somewhat easy. There were some bumps along the way but nothing serious. Then, when I was in my late 50s, the bottom began to fall out. I learned that life's trials are no respecter of age.

In the story of Job in the Old Testament of the Bible, we see a man who was enjoying the favor of God. He had it all – a wife, children, and many material possessions. Some of his neighbors were probably jealous of Job's family and wealth. Then suddenly, his world fell apart around him. He lost everything. Job could not understand what was happening. One day he was enjoying life and the next he was among the ashes (Job 2:8). The Wycliffe Bible translation says he "sat in a dunghill." Dung is another word for manure, and Job was literally in the manure pile.

The story of Job starts with an exchange between God and Satan, who is also known as the "accuser" (Revelation 12:10). Satan says that if God lets down his hedge of protection around Job, he will curse God. Satan tells God that the only reason Job belongs to God is for his wealth. Take the wealth away and Job will curse God. God makes a deal with Satan and removes His protection from Job. This "wager" between God and Satan sets the stage for the remainder of the story.

Once God removes His protection from Job, one messenger after another delivers bad news to Job. The first messenger tells Job the Sabeans "made off" with all his oxen and donkeys (Job 1:14-15). Fire falls and burns up all his sheep and servants (Job 1:16). Next, the Chaldeans take all his camels and kill his servants (Job 1:17). The final messenger tells Job the house collapsed on his children and killed them all (Job 1:18-19). Despite this horrifying news, Job does not curse God.

Satan relentlessly torments Job. In yet another exchange with God, God agrees to allow Satan to inflict sickness on Job's physical body. God prohibits Satan from taking Job's life (Job 2:6). Satan afflicts Job with "painful sores from the soles of his feet to the crown of his head" (Job 2:7). Job ends up on the manure pile but refuses to curse God, even when his wife urges him to "curse God and die" (Job 2:9).

Job's three friends come to offer their support and sympathy. In silence, they sit with him for seven days. When Job breaks the silence, he curses the day he was born (Job 3:1).

Job's friends quickly become his accusers. They tell Job that he must have sin in his life or else he would not be suffering. Job knows he has no sin to confess, but his friends insist that he does. The friend's bad reasoning creates tension between Job and them. They are under the assumption that sin causes suffering.

Violating a law can lead to jail time. In Job's circumstance, however, he had done nothing wrong. Though he knew he had done nothing wrong, he was not able to make sense of his predicament. His friends believed Job had not confessed some unknown sin he had committed. Accusing Job of sin was an easy answer to the harder question of why he was suffering.

Jesus' disciples once questioned Him about the cause of blindness and other physical maladies. Upon encountering a man who had been blind since birth, the disciples asked Jesus, "'Rabbi, who sinned, this man or his parents, that he was born blind?' 'Neither this man nor his parents sinned,' said Jesus, 'but this happened so that the works of God might be displayed in him'" (John 9:2-3). Jesus sheds some light on the reason for suffering: It was so God could display His work (John 9:3). Jesus later healed the blind man and restored his sight. This was the "works of God" displayed in the man.

An acquaintance told me about his experience with a Bible study group he and his wife attended at their church. Their youngest daughter developed a condition that required major surgery. He shared the news of her surgery with the Bible study group and asked for their prayers and support. Those in the group accused him and his wife of having unresolved sin in their lives that gave rise to their daughter's medical condition and resultant surgery.

By accusing him and his wife of sin that caused their daughter's condition, the people in the church responded the same way as Job's friends. This family no longer attends church. Are we any different from Job and his friends thousands of years ago?

In the story of the woman caught in adultery, Jesus gives insight into the way we should treat others.

> The teachers of the law and the Pharisees brought in a woman caught in adultery. They made her stand before the group and said to Jesus, "Teacher, this woman was caught in the act of adultery. In the Law Moses commanded us to stone such women. Now what do you say?" They were using this question as a trap, in order to have a basis for accusing him.
>
> But Jesus bent down and started to write on the ground with his finger. When they kept on questioning him, he straightened up and said to them, "Let any

one of you who is without sin be the first to throw a stone at her." Again he stooped down and wrote on the ground.

At this, those who heard began to go away one at a time, the older ones first, until only Jesus was left, with the woman still standing there. Jesus straightened up and asked her, "Woman, where are they? Has no one condemned you?"

"No one, sir," she said. "Then neither do I condemn you," Jesus declared. "Go now and leave your life of sin."

John 8:3-11

The Mosaic Law of the Old Testament stated that anyone caught in the act of adultery was to be put to death if there were two or more witnesses to the offense (Deuteronomy 17:6). In the case before Jesus, it appears there might have been a lack of witnesses. The woman's accusers were testing Jesus to see what He would do (John 8:6). Jesus challenged her accusers. If any of them had no sin in their life, He said, he could be the one to throw the first stone. Upon hearing these words, they all walked away. Jesus flung a flaming arrow that hit these men right in the heart. They all knew of the sin in their lives. Jesus exposed it. After the accusers left, Jesus did not condemn the woman. He did not give her a 60-minute lecture on the evils of sin. Quite the opposite, all He told her was not to repeat her behavior. God's grace, in the form of Jesus, stepped in. She was on "death row" and received a pardon.

Job had done nothing wrong to deserve what was happening to him. Neither did the couple with the sick child. In both incidents, people treated them as though God were punishing them for a wrong they did not commit. There is a tension here. No one is without sin (Romans 3:23). In our human condition, we all sin. This includes Job and the couple with the sick child. Job's friends and the people in the church group were partially right by saying there was sin in their lives because all of us sin in our humanness. This did not mean that the sufferings of Job and of the couple's daughter were the result of latent sin. Try as all of us may, suffering is going to knock on our door during our stay on earth.

This is an unpleasant fact, even if there is no act of sin to rouse it. Jesus was the only One who can claim to be without sin (1 Peter 1:19). Being without sin, however, did not exempt Him from suffering.

What would have happened if Job's friends had responded to Job with a more loving and supportive approach instead of condemning him? What would have happened if the Bible study group had responded to the girl's parents with love and concern? The outcomes would have been different. Job's suffering would remain, but if the friends had taken a supportive role they would not have added to his despair and feeling of abandonment. If the study group had supported the couple in their time of worry, it would have helped rather than hindered them. In these two scenarios, the accusers display a hint of arrogance. Instead of giving the sufferer the benefit of the doubt, they condemned. They were setting themselves up as judge instead of comforter. It is not the role of the one looking from the outside in to criticize. Only God sees the heart, the inside, of people. A careful approach is best when dealing with those who are suffering so not to compound their pain. This is far better than pursuing and accusing.

As followers of Jesus, we need to take on the supportive non-condemning role when dealing with those who are suffering. I am afraid that this is not always the case, and many have further suffered due to people taking an accusatory role rather a compassionate one. The church should extend the gentle hand of Jesus and not the pointing of a condemning finger.

Why?

I mentioned in a previous chapter that when someone experiences difficult circumstances the question of "Why?" arises. It is in our nature to try to understand why certain things happen. We see innocent children suffering, destruction from natural disasters, and people victimized at the hands of others. These people did nothing wrong to deserve what they are experiencing. We ask why these things happen to the undeserving.

Job asks "Why?" over a dozen times with some heart-wrenching questions. In his desperation, he asks why he was even born (Job 3:11, 10:18). He asks God why He hides His face from him and thinks he is God's enemy (Job 13:24). Job feels abandoned. He is desperate for answers.

Job never learned why he had troubles. Likewise, we may never know why we experience certain things. This may seem unfair, but at times for reasons known only to God He will withhold the "why" from us.

When Jesus was on the cross, He asked, "why have you forsaken me?" (Matthew 27:46). Jesus in His pain and suffering questioned God about the "why." Sometimes I speculate about the magnitude of what Jesus experienced at that moment when He cried out in agony. I do not think we can ever comprehend His pain at that instant.

Is There a Reason for Pain?

Is there an answer to the question of pain? In the confines of this human experience, is there a reason for it? Trying to formulate an answer is not simple.

We all suffer physical pain. For many people cooking on a hot stove has resulted in a burn of some kind. When touching something hot, the nerve sends a signal to the brain that says remove that hand from the source of the pain. In this case, the feeling of pain serves a good purpose. If the feeling of pain were absent, the injury would be much worse.

More than 20 years ago, I experienced the worst physical pain of my life. I had not felt well over the weekend and was at work on a Monday morning. I first thought it was my appendix because the pain was in my right side. Then it moved to my right kidney area. The pain became so intense that I told one of my co-workers that I needed to go to the hospital. During the ride to the hospital, I tried to find a position to relive the pain but failed. The only relief I found was when I received a pain-killing shot from the doctor at the hospital. The doctor determined that I had a kidney stone. I have not experienced pain like that since.

When I have told people about this incident with the kidney stone, they have remarked that it is like the pain of childbirth. My thought was *God bless women* because I do not ever want to go through that again.

I looked to the Bible for answers to the subject of pain. Ironically, I discovered the first reference to pain is about childbearing. This occurs after Adam and Eve disobeyed God and ate the fruit from "the tree in the middle of the garden" (Genesis 3:3). God was not pleased and told Eve, "I will make your pains in childbearing very severe; with painful labor you will give birth to children" (Genesis 3:16). This act of disobedience is what brought on the pain that women experience while birthing a child. This is where pain entered our world.

A woman experiences pain during the birthing process. The only way men can relate to this pain is if they have given an unpleasant "birth" to a kidney stone. Once the woman works through the pain and gives birth, that pain turns to joy upon seeing that new life. Most women affirm that the result was worth going through the pain.

Kidney stones and babies inflict physical pain. What about when we experience emotional pain? This type of pain is not readily visible but can be as bad as or worse than physical pain. We can usually heal from a physical injury, but healing from an emotional injury can take much longer.

I have spoken with people who carry the effect of emotional hurts they suffered as far back as their childhood well into their senior years. As a child, a parent rejected them or did not give them validation. Someone they trusted abused them. There was a betrayal by a close friend. A woman told me that she just wanted someone to believe in her. She is over a half-century old and she continues to look for someone to see value in her. This is traceable back to her childhood when her parents did not give her any reassurance. These are the invisible scars people carry their entire life.

One woman I know grew up with two alcoholic parents. She carried the scars of her childhood into adulthood. Like many others who have faced such traumas, she buried the pain in addictive behavior and alcohol. Many people spend a lifetime dealing with the hurts they suffered as a child. Some try not to deal with the pain and resort to addiction to cover the pain.

People suffer pain through loss. In this life there are a series of losses. As we live, we will experience different types of loss. Suffering begins when we are children and continues through adulthood. I remember the loss of pets when I was a child and the heartache that came with it. As I grew older, I experienced the loss of friends, relationships, and grandparents. More recently, it was the loss of my dad, a marriage, and income. In the story of Job, we see that he suffered a series of losses. Loss is part of our human condition. How we deal with loss makes the difference in how we live. Some who experience the pain of loss may choose to take their life to end the pain. Some turn to addiction. Others decide to place their trust in a higher power knowing there is a God who will help them through their pain. Belief in God not only helps with the pain but adds meaning and purpose to life.

What do we do with pain?

There are two types of pain – physical and emotional. Though they can be separate, they intertwine at numerous intersections. One can affect the other. This is not an uncertain presumption; it is a reality. I know this because it was my reality. I was under such intense emotional strain that the stress began to affect me physically. As I mentioned previously, it caused me pain in my stomach and affected other parts of my body. The stress degraded my immune system to the point that I had difficultly fighting off colds. I had a physical response to my emotional circumstances. I could hide my emotional experience from others, but I was hurting on the inside.

What do we do with pain? How we handle pain reflects how we learned to cope with it as we grew up. Some people run from it. Some get angry at it. Some tolerate it.

Thinking back on the time after Gladys left, I see that I did not handle it well. I was very angry. I expected the divorce because of that series of dreams I had, but I was not exempt from the anger – anger that intensified after I discovered the magnitude of the financial deception. Dealing with the anger was a process and it took time for it to subside.

In the book *Shaking a Fist at God*, Katherine Dell explains that we need to arrive at *a moment of acceptance.*

> What better than to remain calm in the face of suffering and accept it? Acceptance is surely sensible because in fact by the time the suffering has been inflicted, by the time the car accident, for example, has happened, it is too late to do anything about it.[3]

When Job's troubles first began, I do not think he had accepted his dilemma. In fact, it took him all the way to the end of the book before he relented and accepted his circumstance. Likewise, I did not accept all that was happening to me when my difficulty began. I was in it, but that did not mean I liked it or accepted it. Instead, I went kicking and screaming all the way. It took time and processing before I arrived at a place of acceptance. Accepting difficulty and hardship is a process that takes time.

I have heard people use the phrase "it is what it is." Well, although that may be true, it does not mean that someone simply accepts whatever comes along. Jesus struggled the night before He went to the cross.

> "Father, if you are willing, take this cup from me; yet not my will, but yours be done." An angel from heaven appeared to him and strengthened him. And being in anguish, he prayed more earnestly, and his sweat was like drops of blood falling to the ground.
>
> ### *Luke 22:42-44*

The emotional stress Jesus experienced was so severe His sweat was like drops of blood. Though Jesus knew why He had come to this world, He still had a human reaction to His situation. For someone to sweat drops of blood He has to be at the very apex of stress. I have faced people who wanted to kill me, but I have never experienced anything like He did.

Jesus came to the point of acceptance after lamenting what He knew was going to happen. We should follow His example. There are many

---

3. Katherine Dell, *Shaking a Fist at God* (Liguori, MO: Triumph Books, 1995), p. 31.

examples in the Bible of those who accepted their situations. Some accepted death. We can yell, kick, and scream, but that will not change the outcome. At some point there must come a time of acceptance.

> The process of acceptance often results in a new energy to try to bring good out of the suffering. We hear many examples of outstanding human courage and forbearance in our modern world which suggests that the human spirit is not to be crushed. For many people suffering leads eventually to a new strength and will to go on. That is not to say that suffering is good or necessary. It is just that good can come out of it.[4]

An example of good coming from suffering is Jesus' going to the cross for us. He could have refused, but instead He willingly went and embraced His purpose. That was not only acceptance but an act of supreme sacrifice and love.

We may not suffer the pain and loss that Job did, but if we live long enough we will face times of suffering and pain. We may never fully understand why certain things happen to us or to others. Understanding is not a requirement – acceptance of the circumstance is. God knows us and has our best interests at heart. When we accept our difficulty, we will be able to say to God, "Lord, even though I do not understand, I trust You for the outcome."

It was not easy for me to accept what happened. Looking back, I saw that God was removing me from situations to protect me. The experience I had with Jake and the church was a hard lesson for me to take. God removed me from a bad situation to protect me. At first, I was angry after investing so much time toward ordination. Now I can see that God removed me for my own good. It took time, but I did see the "why." Even though it was painful, good did come of it. There was a pony in the manure pile. I just had to wait to find it.

---

4. Katherine Dell, *Shaking a Fist at God* (Liguori, MO: Triumph Books, 1995), p. 32.

To Think About:

1. Have times in your life paralleled those of Job? How did you respond?

2. What if you were accused, like the couple with the sick child, of having sin in your life that caused an illness? How would you respond?

3. Do you know people who resemble the "friends" of Job? How do you handle these "friends"?

4. Have you wrestled with God over suffering or pain in your life? What was the result?

5. Is acceptance of pain or suffering a good response? Can good come from pain and suffering?

11 – Where to Turn

I lift up my eyes to the mountains—where does my help come from? My help comes from the Lord, the Maker of heaven and earth.

Psalm 121:1-2

The story of Job shows the importance of being selective when seeking help. The wrong counsel causes additional harm. Job's friends gave him bad "advice" that only added to his difficulties.

I knew I needed help in my time of crisis. Trying to "tough it out" on my own was a poor choice. I needed someone to listen and to help guide me. I was not sure where to turn. Could I trust someone to keep confidences? Would they be qualified to help? Would they give godly counsel or, like Job's friends, only add to my suffering with condemnation and bad advice?

By this time, the list of people I could trust was small. I could not confide in anyone from my church. Trusted friends who were qualified to help lived far from me. I was at an impasse over what to do. Then I remembered one of my seminary professors who has a counseling practice. I called his office and made an appointment.

Sadly, a certain stigma comes with seeing a psychologist or other mental health professional. Some mistakenly think there is something seriously wrong with seeking help from a therapist and some even think it is a sign of weakness or lack of faith. Those same people see nothing wrong with seeking the help of a medical doctor for physical illnesses or injuries. What's the difference? Why should a person experiencing emotional pain not go to someone for counsel during difficult times? As discussed in the last chapter, emotional stress affects physical wellbeing. So why not attempt to take care of the emotional issue before it becomes a physical issue?

I first sought counseling two weeks after Gladys left. I needed help with grief over the loss of my dad. It had been two and a half years since his passing, and I was still "stuck" in certain areas of my life.

Anticipating my first counseling session was unnerving. What if people found out I was going to a "shrink"? I put aside my pride and stopped worrying about what others thought. I was doing this for me and no one else. I wanted help in getting through something I could not get through on my own. Just as I would seek a qualified professional to help with a broken bone, so I was seeking a qualified professional to help with a broken heart.

I was not sure what to expect my first visit. I knew what I had seen in movies and on television. The patient lay on a big leather sofa while speaking with a psychologist. I had never done this before. What should I expect? Would I have to lie on a couch? Would I have to confess things I did as a child? Would I have to talk about my father and mother?

During my first session, I found that my apprehensions were groundless. I did not lie on a couch. My fears of shock therapy or receiving a prefrontal lobotomy were unfounded. I sat in a chair and explained my concerns to the psychologist.

I continued in counseling for two and half years. Initially we met once a week and later tapered to once a month. After my dad's death, I confronted divorce, betrayal by a spouse, betrayal by leadership in the church, and bankruptcy. It was no accident that God had me speaking to a counselor. I was going through counseling while dealing with most of these issues. I had a counselor helping me along a difficult path, just as I helped others in my role as a chaplain.

Keep in mind that counseling has limitations. Counseling leads a person to a plateau that is much better than where they started. After counseling reaches this point, this is not the end for those who follow Jesus because God continues the healing process.

Get into the "Word"

It is not possible to place enough emphasis on the necessity of prayer and Bible study. This should not be a matter of when one "feels" like it. Instead, this should be a daily discipline. Statistics on the number of people in America who read their Bible are very disturbing. Caleb Bell reports in an online article that 57% read the Bible four or fewer times per year and 26% read the Bible four or more times a week.[5] This means that only 26 out of every 100 people read the Bible with any regularity. If these numbers came from a survey of the general population, it is no wonder why we are experiencing an epidemic of spiritual anemia in America. If these numbers came from a survey of church attendees, the numbers are even more alarming. Either scenario is an area for concern given that only 26% of people are reading the Bible frequently.

I developed a daily time of study and prayer over the past 42 years. This daily discipline is a source of help that has guided me through many difficult times. The Bible is a manual for life. It gives direction in the way we should live.

Look at it this way. Each state and even some municipalities have laws that govern the roadways. Yet they vary state-to-state or maybe even city-to-city. In the United States, we all know to drive in the right lane or lanes no matter what direction we are going. Signs and traffic lights show us when to stop, yield, and slow down. Failure to follow these laws can result in an accident or a citation.

Some do not abide by traffic laws because apparently they wish to create their own rules. They exceed speed limits, fail to stop completely for stop signs, and speed up to make it through traffic signals turning red. They are endangering not only themselves but others. The outcome of this behavior can be costly. It does not have to be this way, if only they were willing to follow the laws.

Those who choose not to read the Bible drive aimlessly through life hoping that in the end they will arrive at a destination of spiritual bliss. There are no rules to go by and no regard for warning signs. They

---

5. Bell, Caleb, *Poll: Americans Love the Bible but Don't Read It Much*, Religious News Service, April 4, 2013.
http://religionnews.com/2013/04/04/poll-americans-love-the-bible-but-dont-read-it-much/.

make up the rules as they go along. There are no reference points or directional signs along the way. It is like trying to drive to a destination in a distant city while blindfolded.

A person who reads and studies the Bible learns there is a set of standards to guide the way. Just like traffic laws, there are certain safeguards in place to help and protect. There are signs and warnings and reference points on the road of life. These people can see and have a clear sense of direction.

One Sunday morning at church the pastor taught on Job. He said that Job lost everything including his wife. Most in the congregation missed the error, and the error did not negate the point of the teaching. But Job did not lose his wife. If she was dead how could she have told Job to "curse God and die" (Job 2:9)? Without a regimen of Bible study, we are gullible and easily misled.

In *The Craft of Christian Teaching*, Israel Galindo stresses the importance of knowing the content and context.

> "There was a man of the Pharisees named Nicodemus who went to Jericho by night. And he fell upon stony ground and the thorns choked him half to death.
>
> "The next morning Solomon and his wife, Gomorrah, came by and they took him down to the ark so that Moses could care for him. But as he was going through the eastern gate toward the ark, his hair was caught in a limb, and he hung there forty days and forty nights. Afterward he was hungry and the ravens came and fed him.
>
> "The next day three wise men came and carried him down to the boat dock, where he caught a ship to Nineveh. When he got there, he saw Delilah sitting on a wall.
>
> "And Nicodemus said, 'Throw her down off the wall.' And the wise men said, 'How many times shall we throw her down? Seven times seven?' And Nicodemus replied, 'Nay, but seventy times seven?' And they threw her down 490 times. She burst asunder in their midst, and they picked up twelve baskets of

fragments. My question is: 'Whose wife will she be in the resurrection?'"[6]

This humorous account addresses those who teach in addition to those who listen, watch, or read. All the story elements are from the Bible, of course, but they are taken out of context. It is like putting words in a bag, shaking it, and pouring them out on a table. The right words are there, but they are completely out of order. Content needs context and verification. The way to verify content is to know the subject. Learning the subject comes from diligent study.

Reading the Bible was my encouragement when going through my difficulties. I was under a lot of stress, and the study of scripture helped me along the way. I lost count of how many times I read Psalm 91. My mom calls this her "9-1-1" chapter. I love the words the psalmist penned in these verses. It speaks of the protection that God gives. Even if times are tough, He is there. It assures us that God is our refuge and strength. The writer encourages us that no matter how terrible the circumstance, God is there to deflect attacks and deliver His people from harm. There is safety for those who trust Him.

Many biblical stories show that life is not always "smooth sailing." In the story of Jesus' calming the storm, Jesus gave "orders to cross to the other side of the lake" (Matthew 8:18).

> Then he got into the boat and his disciples followed him. Suddenly a furious storm came up on the lake, so that the waves swept over the boat. But Jesus was sleeping. The disciples went and woke him, saying, "Lord, save us! We're going to drown!" He replied, "You of little faith, why are you afraid?" Then he got up and rebuked the winds and the waves, and it was completely calm. The men were amazed and asked, "What kind of man is this? Even the winds and the waves obey him!"
>
> ***Matthew 8:23-27***

---

6. Israel Galindo, *The Craft of Christian Teaching* (Valley Forge, PA: Judson Press, 1998), p. 78-79.

This story is a goldmine of applications for life. Jesus gave the order to cross the lake. When Jesus said "cross to the other side of the lake," that meant they were going to safely arrive at the other side. He would not tell them to do something that was not going to happen. They obeyed Him and got into the boat and set out across the water. Some of the disciples were experienced fishermen, so this was not their first time on these waters. If the storm was so intense that it upset these men, it had to be horrific. Where was Jesus during all the commotion? He was asleep in the boat. While His disciples were in panic mode, Jesus slept peacefully. These were two very different reactions to the same situation.

After they awoke Jesus, He admonished them for their lack of faith. He reprimanded the disciples *before* He calmed the storm. Now He could have calmed the storm and then rebuked the disciples, but I think He was making a point. He slept during the storm and was not afraid. I think He wanted to show the disciples that there was no reason for fear. Jesus told them to go to the other side of the lake. When He said they were going to the other side of the lake, this was a guarantee. Jesus would not tell them to do something and not follow through. Since Jesus told them to go, it was up to the disciples to trust that they would get there. In the end, they arrived safely at the other side of the lake, just as He had said (Matthew 8:28).

What can we take away from this story? The storm can represent our difficulties in life. Sometimes they occur suddenly, with no warning. The storm was so violent the disciples believed they would perish. I cannot imagine how they felt when they saw Jesus sound asleep while the waves were crashing against the boat. They probably thought He was out of touch with reality. "Then He got up and rebuked the winds and the waves and it was completely calm" (Matthew 8:26). Jesus spoke and all was peaceful. The power in His words calmed a terrible storm. If Jesus can harness a "furious" storm in nature, He can bind the storms in our lives.

Amazingly, I did not lose any sleep during my season of trouble. Though I experienced horrible stress, I had no problem with rest. When I lay down at night, a God-given peace allowed me to get the proper sleep. It is not easy to explain why. Though I was under stress, I was not worried. Jesus told the people, "Therefore do not worry about tomorrow, for tomorrow will worry about itself. Each day has enough trouble of its own" (Matthew 6:34). If Jesus says not to worry, then His followers should take Him at His Word and not worry. I believe the Lord's words were the source of my peace and a good night's sleep.

Should we *never* be afraid? It is human to fear. We are naturally afraid of a perceived threat or impending danger. Everyone has the fight-or-flight response to certain threatening situations. If someone comes at us with a club and means to do us harm, we instinctively leave the threat or confront it directly. A healthy fear helps us avoid injury or harm. When fear keeps us from performing certain functions, however, the fear is not healthy.

I experienced two near-drowning incidents in my youth. The first happened on a family vacation in Texas. We were at a lake, and I had not yet learned to swim. I was on a boat dock wearing a life jacket. My dad said, "Jump in," so I jumped in – and went straight to the bottom. The water was over my head. The life jacket had not done its job in keeping me afloat. I do not remember who rescued me. I think it was my dad. Over the years I have joked about this saying that my dad tried to get rid of me. At the time, though, it was not funny.

The second incident occurred when I was working at a golf and hunting club while in high school. I had learned to swim by then. We swam in a large pond at the club. The two teenage sons of the club owner and I took a boat out to the middle of the pond. While swimming, I became entangled in a rope. I was under the water fighting my way back to the surface. The older son saw me struggling and pulled me to the surface. I might not be alive today if he had not pulled me to safety.

I developed a fear of drowning in response to these situations. I remember those times of terror whenever I see a movie or show that depicts someone going under the surface of the water.

Another time I was on a fishing trip with two friends when a "furious storm" approached in the distance. We were on the water at the opposite side of the lake from the boat ramp. We scrambled to reach the boat ramp before the storm hit, but we were too late. The storm hit with all its fury. The strong wind generated waves that engulfed the boat.

The rain was a torrential downpour. To add to the chaos, lightning was striking all around us. The boat was barely making headway into the strong headwind. The ramp seemed miles away. At last, we reached the ramp, soaked but intact.

I share this story to explain what I was feeling while on the water that day. We were in danger. The boat was the highest point on the water, which made the three of us potential lightning rods. But I had a peace that all would be well during the ordeal. It was a supernatural "peace that transcends all understanding" (Philippians 4:7).

Over the years my apprehensions about drowning subsided. I believe this stems from my trust in a higher power. When I made a commitment to God, my life changed. I realized that I do not have much control over what happens to me. Believing in God means trusting Him for the outcome no matter the situation. In my career in law enforcement, I faced many life-and-death situations. When going into those situations, I had to trust God for the outcome. I could not let the thought of dying prevent me from doing my job. This applied also to being in a boat on waters that could consume me. I cannot let those past experiences deter me from doing something I love to do – like fishing.

Jesus was in the boat with the disciples during the entire storm. Yet He did not react like the disciples. Jesus knew very well what was to transpire on the lake. It was test time for the disciples. It was a pop quiz in "Faith 101." The Teacher was in the boat with them, and this was a hands-on classroom experience. What was the purpose of this testing? It was preparing them for their future. They needed to learn to trust in Jesus no matter the circumstances. They also needed to see who Jesus is – the One who can control a storm.

For the beginner or someone who has not read the Bible for some time, a good place to start is in the Gospels: Matthew, Mark, Luke, and John. These four books are the heart of the Bible because they record the life, death, and resurrection of Jesus. Jesus became the Savior of humanity and laid the foundation for the church.

I encourage everyone to read and study independently. Going to church on Sunday and listening to a sermon does *not* qualify as study any more than watching an instructional video on appendectomies makes one a surgeon. I tell people to study and verify what they hear. It makes no difference if it is your neighbor, your pastor, or a television preacher. The only way to know if you are hearing the truth is to study the Bible and learn its contents. The knowledge gained through study will equip you to discern when you hear something that does not align with God's Word.

When reading the Word, ask yourself: "How do these words apply to me?" Application is a part of study. For example, The Bible teaches that sex outside of marriage is wrong. When someone who is involved in this activity reads this teaching, he or she needs to decide "Am I going to continue in this behavior or am I going to adhere to the biblical teaching?" The Bible clearly states it is wrong. If a person continues in this behavior, he or she does so knowing that it is contradictory to the Bible. The right choice is not to engage in this activity any further. This is applying the Word to one's life. The Word is a guide to a better way of life.

Talking to God

We should have a daily prayer time in addition to daily Bible study. Prayer is a time of focus and reenergizing. Picture yourself as a rechargeable battery. Look at praying as plugging into the power source – God. Over time, a battery will go dead if it is not recharged. If we do not "plug in" for recharging, we will grow spiritually depleted. Therefore, it is imperative that we plug into the "energy source" each day. This assures that the battery will remain charged. A charged battery is stronger and more proficient.

Not praying daily is like filling the gas tank of a car in Los Angeles and trying to drive to New York City without stopping for gas. Even if we set up the car for minimum fuel usage, the car will not make it to the east coast with any sized gas tank that is practical. This same principle applies to daily prayer. Begin to see prayer as a source of fuel for powering spiritual life. Without that fuel, there is no forward motion, no spiritual growth.

What is prayer? Prayer is talking to God. The Bible gives guidance in how we should pray. One of the first examples of how to pray is from Jesus in His Sermon on the Mount.

> "This, then, is how you should pray: 'Our Father in
> heaven, hallowed be your name, your kingdom come,
> your will be done, on earth as it is in heaven. Give us
> today our daily bread. And forgive us our debts, as we
> also have forgiven our debtors. And lead us not into
> temptation, but deliver us from the evil one.'"

Matthew 6:9-13

This is called "The Lord's Prayer." It is a model prayer. It shows how to honor God, ask for daily provision, forgive, and request help in not being led astray by the enemy of the soul. This is not the only example Jesus gave in how to pray.

In John 17, Jesus prays throughout the chapter. In the beginning of the chapter, He prays for Himself (John 17:1-5). Next, He prays for His disciples (John 17:6-18). Then He prays for all believers (John 17:20-26). So in our prayers we can pray for those around us as well as for ourselves.

Why is prayer necessary? Imagine any relationship without communication. If there is no communication, there is no relationship. Friends who do not speak to one another will probably not be friends for long. The same applies to prayer. It is engaging conversation with the Heavenly Father. Prayer maintains our relationship with God, so prayer is necessary. Keeping in communication with God is an essential part of a relationship with Him. The Bible teaches that the followers of God should pray without ceasing (1 Thessalonians 5:17).

The Bible also teaches how followers should *not* pray. "And when you pray, do not be like the hypocrites, for they love to pray standing in the synagogues and on the street corners to be seen by others. Truly I tell you, they have received their reward in full" (Matthew 6:5). Jesus continues: "But when you pray, go into your room, close the door and pray to your Father, who is unseen. Then your Father, who sees what is done in secret, will reward you" (Matthew 6:6). Some people are very eloquent and have a way with words. This can make others who do not speak as well feel inadequate. God is not impressed with eloquent speech. He is concerned about authenticity of heart.

When is a good time to pray? Although prayer can take place anytime or anywhere, it is wise to develop a consistent time of prayer.

Find a time when interruptions are at a minimum. Prayer becomes a part of the day with a set schedule.

The amount of time spent in prayer depends upon the person. There is no time limit! I have heard people say that they spend hours every day in prayer. This may be true, but for most of us this is not feasible. Most people cannot stay focused for 15 minutes. There are days when I take 15–20 minutes to pray and others when I spend over a half an hour. In times of an emergency, we might only have time for a short one-second prayer: "Help!" Under normal circumstances, there are no time limits. What is important is developing communication with God and a relationship with Him.

Prayer is not backing up a dump truck load of requests and concerns, dumping them, and then driving off. Praying is also listening. Luke tells us that Mary sat at the feet of Jesus listening (Luke 10:39). Jesus said she chose *the better thing* (Luke 10:42). By not taking the time to listen, we may miss answers and opportunities.

Sometimes hearing God is difficult. Maybe at times He seems distant and silent. Remember the story of the disciples in the boat with Jesus. They thought they were doomed as Jesus slept. Jesus probably seemed distant and silent to them, but He was right there with them the whole time. He did not let them perish. He kept silent until the right moment and then acted. He will do the same for everyone who will trust Him to act at the appropriate time.

To Think About:

1. Have you ever thought about going to counseling? Did you go or not, and why?

2. How much time do you spend in Bible study? What can you do to improve your study time in the Bible?

3. Are you praying daily? If not, how can you improve your prayer life?

12 – More Than Just Surviving

The thief comes only to steal and kill and destroy; I have come that they may have life, and have it to the full.

John 10:10

A friend and I were on a hunting trip in the tundra of the Alaskan Peninsula. Two bush planes dropped us off with all our gear near the edge of a lakebed where we made camp. There was nothing around except the green vastness and some scattered brushy areas – no trees. Walking across the tundra was like venturing across 10-inch-thick wet shag carpet; the going was slow and difficult.

One evening as we were heading back to camp, it was late and darkness overtook us. We were in a predicament. Should we continue and risk injury from walking in the dark, or should we spend the night in the cold dampness? Rather than risk injury, we spent the night away from the comfort of camp. We made a shelter in a brushy area with only a poncho and bungee cords. This was grizzly bear country, I had no desire to become a snack for the local bears. We were in survival mode. I sat up all night while my friend slept at my side. Watching for bears was more important than sleep. The dawn came; we survived the night.

This was a true survival experience. That part of the world is unforgiving. Preparation for worst-case scenarios was essential to remain alive. Thankfully, we had read and studied before the trip so we understood how to survive a night away from camp.

Though most people will not experience what we did, all of us will have "wilderness" experiences in our lives. There will be times when we feel that we are just surviving. The key to survival is preparation. If my friend and I had not prepared and studied prior to our trip, we might not have survived that night in the Alaskan wilderness.

Trying to prepare for the unexpected is not easy. How does anyone prepare for the "messes" in life? What if a family member suddenly dies, a job is lost, or a marriage collapses? Is there anything that can lessen the effects of these life-shattering events? I do not think any amount of preparation will cushion the initial impact of any traumatic episode. There is simply no way to prepare for receiving the news that you or a loved one has a terminal illness. Receiving this type of report is like a hard punch to the gut that knocks the breath out of us.

When going through my "real life" wilderness experience, I did not feel prepared. I had never experienced the death of a parent, divorce, or financial loss. I did not know what to expect until I went through the events and trials. I felt much better prepared for that night spent away from camp in Alaska than I did for what happened to me at home.

I learned while going through these experiences. I did not know what to expect after my dad died or when I was going through a divorce or entering bankruptcy. Experience is sometimes a harsh teacher. In retrospect, I now have better knowledge of what to anticipate in certain circumstances. These are additional tools in my bag of life experiences, tools that also help me in ministering to others when they face difficult times.

I received training to deal with those who are facing traumatic events. When counseling people who have been through a distressing situation, I advise them about the sorts of things they might experience. Not everyone reacts the same way to the same situation. What I do is prepare them for possible aftereffects. Some may experience subsequent disturbances and some may not. People react differently. A police officer with 10 years on the job will react differently than an officer who is fresh out of the training academy. My goal is to prepare those I counsel for possible future issues that can occur after involvement in a traumatic situation.

How can a person prepare for the unexpected? Studying scripture is a good place to start. The Bible is a treasure of information on the "how to" of life. In addition to the Bible are many books that deal with specific topics such as grief, divorce, and personal spiritual growth. If you belong to a church, check to see if they have any resources available.

In addition to reading, seek someone trustworthy with whom to share. Sometimes all it takes is someone who will listen. Find a "safe" support group to join. Though group settings are not comfortable for everyone, they can be helpful because in groups people discover they are not alone, not the only person who has had their type of experience. These settings can offer support and encouragement. Use caution when getting involved with a group, however. Remember the story of that couple whose Bible study group blamed them for their little girl's illness? Be wary: If there is a hint of something amiss, stay away from that person or group.

During my searches for answers, I found a book that caught my attention – *Moving Forward After Divorce*. It shed light on my experience. In one story recounted in the book, Meg's husband walked out. "'Running away is immature. How many ways can we say that?' wonders Meg's counselor. 'Abandoning your spouse is taking the easy way out.'"[7] Meg experienced pain and heartbreak when her husband abandoned her. She discovered that her husband's leaving was his immaturity and not because of her actions. Her husband was not willing to work on the relationship; he took the easy way out. Meg's situation is very much like mine.

The authors of the book, David and Lisa Frisbie, are interested in gardening. What makes a garden grow? The answer, of course, is "manure." They advise us: "Try viewing the 'manure' of divorce as the fertilizer for your new self." They go on to say, "You'll discover that this paradigm shift is deeply rooted in the soil of a puzzling reality: adversity and hardship enrich your life in ways you might not have sought."[8]

Going through a divorce was challenging. The process took months and demanded much of my attention. This was the beginning of a new chapter in my life. There were adjustments I had to make. I had to fill the voids left by a *former* spouse. The duties she performed in the home

---

7. David and Lisa Frisbie, *Moving Forward After Divorce* (Eugene, OR: Harvest House Publishers, 2006), p. 20.

8. Ibid, 54.

became mine. I learned that I could do it. I survived the distress, pain, and anger of divorce. Divorce was only one portion of my circumstances. I survived all of it, and I have grown in the process. God took a pile of manure and turned it in to something positive.

One of my favorite movie scenes is in *Facing the Giants*. During a high school football practice, the coach picked one of the best players, Brock, to perform the hated "death crawl." One player gets down on his hands and feet and crawls while carrying another player on his back. Usually the player crawling collapses after travelling 30–50 yards. This time, the coach blindfolded Brock. As he proceeded down the field, the coach yelled, "Don't quit! Don't quit!" Brock's muscles looked as if they would give out at any moment. The coach continued to push him. Finally, Brock could no longer move forward and collapsed to the ground exhausted. Then the coach told him to take off the blindfold. Brock was amazed to see that he had traveled the length of the entire field – 100 yards!

What Brock saw in himself is not what the coach saw in him. The coach could see Brock's potential. He had the perspective of one looking from the outside in. This is better than one looking from the inside out. All of us can see the good or bad in others much more easily than we can see them in ourselves. From the coach's vantage, he could see what Brock had to offer. From Brock's viewpoint, he could not see what the coach saw in him. All he could see was his limitations.

Brock's story is an example of what a positive influence can do. Pushed to the limit, he was out of his comfort zone and could not imagine traveling the entire length of the field. Brock was fortunate to have someone – his coach – who looked for the best in the players. This is not always the case. Some coaches see only the worst in their players. This can also apply in other relationships where someone sees only the negative in another. If someone does not match their expectations, they may label the person *not good enough*.

Many people let others dictate their potential. Maybe a grade school teacher said, "You'll never amount to anything." Maybe a parent made a child feel he or she could never do anything right. Maybe a boss promoted someone less qualified. There are many scenarios in which denial of potential takes place, but the common result is a person who felt he could never measure up to the standards of another and who never realizes his full capability. No one should allow another to dictate his or her possibilities. God is the One who gives people certain abilities. Brock had a coach who was wise enough to bring out the best in him.

Guard the Mind

Our mind is where the battle is raging. It is the battlefield where a conflict between good and evil takes place. This battle will continue until death takes us. The Apostle Paul had this struggle: "I do not understand what I do. For what I want to do I do not do, but what I hate I do" (Romans 7:15). Paul's experience was the same as our experience now.

Every act begins as a thought. It makes no difference whether it is the choice of what clothes to wear or what to eat or whom to marry – it began in the mind. The Bible makes numerous references to the mind because the authors of the Bible knew the importance of the mind. A person's mind is in one of two places – living according to the flesh or living according to the Spirit.

When the Bible refers to the flesh, it is speaking of those who are living by their own thinking and desires and consider whatever they feel is right in their mind to be acceptable and permissible. A person who is living by the Spirit lives according to biblical teachings and God's leading.

> Those who live according to the flesh have their minds set on what the flesh desires; but those who live in accordance with the Spirit have their minds set on what the Spirit desires. The mind governed by the flesh is death, but the mind governed by the Spirit is life and peace.
>
> ***Romans 8:5-6***

Those who have received Jesus in their lives are living in accordance with the Spirit. All others are living in accordance with the flesh, or living according to their own regulation. When a person invites Jesus into his or her life there is a spiritual birth (John 3:1-21) and a renewing of the mind (Romans 12:2). This involves a change of focus. The focus that was on the things of this life is now on Jesus and an eternal afterlife.

When describing the armor of God, Paul spoke of the helmet of salvation (Ephesians 6:17). A soldier puts on a helmet to protect the head. The helmet that Paul was referring to is one of a spiritual nature. A helmet of salvation protects the mind. In Christendom, salvation keeps us from sin. Sin is a wrongdoing, a trespass against God's law.

Ears and eyes are the avenues by which information enters the mind (Matthew 6:22). What enters the mind influences how people act and think. If a person continually listens to music with violent content and watches movies or shows that glorify violence and promiscuous living, how will he or she behave in the future? It is the old adage: garbage-in, garbage-out. Be diligent in protecting your mind from negative influences. This is especially true of impressionable young minds.

Parents with young children need to monitor what their children listen to and watch. Some music, movies, and television shows contain excessive violence. Children are too young to grasp the difference between what is reality and what is make-believe. Repeated exposure to violence can cause children to act out on what they see and hear. Some may see no harm in exposing their children to anything with violent content. Then they are aghast when their "little angel" is chasing the neighbor's cat down the street trying to set it on fire. If there is any doubt as to what a child is listening to or watching, take the cautious approach and eliminate it.

> "No one lights a lamp and puts it in a place where it will be hidden, or under a bowl. Instead they put it on its stand, so that those who come in may see the light. Your eye is the lamp of your body. When your eyes are healthy, your whole body also is full of light. But when they are unhealthy, your body also is full of darkness. See to it, then, that the light within you is not darkness. Therefore, if your whole body is full of light, and no part of it dark, it will be just as full of light as when a lamp shines its light on you."
>
> *Luke 11:33-36*

Jesus spoke these words to warn us to pay attention to what comes into the mind through the eyes. If something is questionable, we need to consider eliminating it.

I attended a men's conference several years ago. The speaker spoke about pornography. At the end of his presentation, he invited those who are struggling with the issue to come forward if they wanted help. Of the more than 200 men there, three quarters went forward. These men allowed something into their minds that had a grip on them. This was a revelation about how important it is to guard the mind.

Other People

People are social creatures. Most of us desire interaction with other people and like being around others. That is a good thing because reaching out is a great way to get your mind off personal issues. Sitting around alone and dwelling on problems is not productive.

How does one become involved with other people? One way is to ask a pastor if he or she knows someone who needs help. Find someone at church or at work who needs a friend. Many people love socializing over a cup of coffee or another common activity. When we invest time and interest in another person, it helps to relieve the burden of our own concerns. It also gives us an opportunity to share. Sharing our burdens with others is a biblical principle (Galatians 6:2). We are not to carry our troubles alone. Sharing will help to lighten the load.

One summer I led a senior group at a church. I had a blast with these older people. We played games, watched movies, ate, and studied the Bible. At one meeting, the women in the group came in laughing with funny tales about their recent visit to a horse track. I could only picture this group of feisty grayed-haired women at the track, urging their favorite horse to run faster and suggesting that all the others should just get out of its way.

Staying involved with others helped me. I did not focus on my situation but on helping others. I did not want to fall into the trap of feeling sorry for myself. That is an easy thing to do when we are going through a bad situation.

Richard was a very energetic World War II veteran. His energy was contagious. Being around him made people feel better. He was part of the landing forces in France on D-Day. During the landing, a piece of shrapnel struck him in the back of the neck. He suffered major hearing loss among other serious injuries, and they transferred him to a military hospital back here in the United States.

When he was in the hospital, he never left his bed because he felt sorry for himself. One day he saw two women walk into that room full of wounded soldiers. The duo went bed-to-bed speaking to everyone. One of the two was Helen Keller, the famous deaf and blind woman. She overcame tremendous obstacles in her life to become who she was. After Richard met her, he said that he had "no darn reason to be feeling sorry for myself."

This encounter was life changing for Richard. He realized that feeling sorry for himself would not get him anywhere. He made a choice not to live in self-pity. The encounter with Helen Keller changed his perspective. After seeing the adversity she overcame and how she was reaching out to help him and his wounded comrades, he knew he had no reason to complain.

In Richard's situation, he had to make a choice: Was he going to live in self-pity or was he going to move forward? His encounter with Helen Keller helped to push him ahead. Remember this when you are facing adversity: There are choices. Will you stay and wallow in the manure or will you move ahead?

Got To Let It Go

Many livestock have a permanent mark left on them by a hot iron. The hot iron burns a permanent mark of a brand into the animal's hide that identifies the owner. Though the livestock recover from the initial contact of the hot iron, a brand-shaped scar remains.

People recover from hurt, but scars linger. The memories of past hurts can last a lifetime. Think back to when you were a child. Can you recall an occasion when someone said or did something that hurt you? Chances are you can. That memory remains vivid in the mind. There are hurts more recent than childhood, but no matter when they occur, they remain.

When I was five years old, I would meet the school bus at the end of our driveway. On one occasion during winter, the frozen tire ruts were exceptionally difficult to navigate, and thus I slipped and fell numerous times while walking toward the bus. My feet had no traction on the ice. I could hear students on the bus laughing at me as I made that seemingly endless journey to the waiting yellow monster. I was humiliated and embarrassed. This occurred 58 years ago, but it remains in my mind. The hurt from the humiliation and embarrassment I felt that day lasted many years. Although the hurt is gone, the memory remains. Releasing the hurts of the past does not erase the memories but it does remove the sting of the hurts.

Prior hurts can bind us like chains if we cannot let them go. For example, chains secure heavy loads on large trucks. Steel chains prevent movement of whatever they hold. Past hurts can bind and prevent movement. These "chains" are strong, but they can be broken.

Some people refuse to give up past hurts. It is as if they get some satisfaction in hanging on to the hurts and refusing to let them go. I think part of the reason for this refusal is the feeling of injustice. No one likes unfair treatment, especially when it is unwarranted. We think that releasing the hurt means the offender gets away unpunished.

Fear is another factor in not letting go. If a person lets go of the hurt, nothing else takes its place. Yet not letting go is like trying to swim with a 100-pound weight strapped around our waist. No matter how hard the swimmer tries, he will not stay afloat but only sink to the bottom. Letting go of past hurts sets us free because the chains that bound us are now broken.

How can we let go of past hurts? "Cast your cares on the Lord and he will sustain you; he will never let the righteous be shaken" (Psalm 55:22). Jesus told us, "Come to me, all you who are weary and burdened, and I will give you rest" (Matthew 11:28). These verses are saying that God can handle hurts better than we can. The chains are the hurts. Turning them over to God breaks those chains. It is up to the person holding the hurt to turn it over to God. If someone holds on to the hurt, the chains will bind.

A Double-Edged Sword

The writers of the Bible refer to it as a weapon. In Hebrews 4:12, the Word of God is described as "sharper than any double-edged sword."

A sword is a tool used in battle and its purpose is to defeat the enemy. An army does not go to war to be defeated but to prevail. God's people may not be on a physical battlefield, but they are certainly in a spiritual battle. In the spiritual realm, the Bible refers to the enemy as Satan, the devil, the serpent, the dragon, or the evil one. Different names that all refer to the same enemy. The enemy is the opposite of God. God is light. The enemy represents darkness and is the "father of lies" (John 8:44).

> Be alert and of sober mind. Your enemy the devil prowls around like a roaring lion looking for someone to devour.
>
> *1 Peter 5:8*

How can an unseen enemy be defeated? In Jesus' day, the New Testament, the Bible books from Matthew through Revelation had not yet been written. Jesus and the people used the writings that make up the Old Testament of the Bible.

Jesus was without food for 40 days when Satan came to Him. Satan challenged Jesus at every level. He questioned who Jesus was: "If you are the Son of God, tell these stones to become bread" (Matthew 4:3). This shows that Satan will stop at nothing to discourage followers of Jesus. Jesus fought Satan in His wilderness experience by using words from the book of Deuteronomy (Matthew 4:1-13). Jesus replied to all the attacks by quoting verses from the Old Testament. Using Bible verses in this way is an example for everyone. The Bible is a weapon to use against a ruthless foe.

What can one take away from Jesus' experience in the wilderness? Jesus had a wilderness incident. He experienced many of the same things that we all do in life. Jesus was tempted. Satan knows what is in the Bible and how to use it against us. Satan also knew to tempt Jesus when He was tired and hungry. This is when people are most vulnerable. Jesus countered everything that Satan attempted to use against Him by saying "it is written." Jesus masterfully used the written Word of God to oppose Satan's attacks.

If the enemy confronted Jesus, His followers can expect the same. They are not exempt from the attacks. Jesus gave the example of how to use the Bible as a defense against those attacks. Followers must arm themselves with knowledge to take up the defense.

Obey

Another way not to "just survive" is through obedience to God and His Word. If one truly desires to do God's will, it requires obedience. Obedience is not easy and may necessitate sacrifice.

Noah is one of the most prominent characters of the Bible. During Noah's day, God was not pleased with the wickedness of the people. They became so corrupt that God regretted creating them (Genesis 6:5-8). God decided to destroy the earth and all its corruption. Noah was a good man in God's sight, and God told him to build an ark (Genesis 6:14-22). Noah obeyed and began the enormous task. Imagine the ridicule he received during the 120-year construction process! There was no water in the area for a boat. People thought that he was crazy for building a boat on dry land. His focus was on the mission that God set before him not on a public opinion poll.

Noah's obedience resulted in his and his family's avoiding the fate of those who chose not to follow the ways of God. If Noah had not obeyed God, his family would not have survived, and no animals would have survived. His obedience saved humanity and the animals. Think about the consequences if Noah had refused to obey.

Obedience is difficult and it can be costly. God looks for those who are willing to hear and do. "My sheep listen to my voice; I know them, and they follow me" (John 10:27). If one is to survive, obedience to God and His Word is crucial.

Things Do Not Measure Up

People tend to compare themselves to others. Why did he get to do that? Or: Why am I struggling while she has everything?

> I know what it is to be in need, and I know what it is to have plenty. I have learned the secret of being content in any and every situation, whether well fed or hungry, whether living in plenty or in want.
>
> ***Philippians 4:12***

The Apostle Paul was expressing how he had learned to be content in every situation. When he wrote the book of Philippians, he was living under guard in Rome awaiting trial (Acts 28:30). Paul knew adversity. What was the source of his contentment? I believe he had learned to see his situations with eternal eyes. Paul had the most radical conversion of anyone (Acts 9). His personal encounter with Jesus changed the course of his life. He went from being a persecutor to a follower of Jesus and beyond that, an apostle who wrote about half of the books in the New Testament! Paul's focus moved from the "right now" temporal to the eternal – the temporal being his fleeting earthly existence. He was not dwelling on what was happening to him in the present but was looking to a promised future.

After Paul became a follower of Jesus, he experienced shipwrecks, beatings, imprisonment, and pursuit by angry mobs. He knew persecution. His life turned from the persecutor to the persecuted. No matter what happened to his physical body, he had a future home in Heaven. This is the source of contentment, the assurance of an eternal place in a heavenly home.

Until one has a personal encounter with Jesus, the assurance of a place in Heaven is not possible. Many people know about Jesus but have not accepted Him as Lord and Savior of their life. Having knowledge of Jesus and *knowing* Jesus are not the same.

This is the key to unlocking everything we have discussed and not just surviving. The key is getting to know Jesus at a personal level. This is simple to do, but very hard. All we have to do is invite Him into our heart.

In my early church days, at the end of every church service there was an invitation for people to go forward and accept Jesus into their lives. Ushers came to the people standing in the congregation and invited them to follow them to the front of the sanctuary. I remember standing one Sunday morning with a death grip on the back of the wooden pew in front of me. One of those attendants came and tried to get me to go forward. There was no way I was letting go of that pew. I was not ready to commit, and it would have taken the Jaws of Life to get my hands off that pew. That is what I mean when I say that it is simple but very hard to do.

"Here I am! I stand at the door and knock. If anyone hears my voice and opens the door, I will come in and eat with that person, and they with me" (Revelation 3:20). A painting depicts Jesus standing at a door knocking. Upon close inspection, we see that there is no handle on the outside of the door. The artist purposely left the handle out of the painting. The door opens only from the inside. The door represents a person's heart. When Jesus knocks at the door of the heart, it is up to the person to open the door and let Him in.

Jesus told Nicodemus, "no one can see the kingdom of God unless they are born again" (John 3:3). Nicodemus did not understand because he was thinking of physical birth.

> Jesus answered, "Very truly I tell you, no one can enter the kingdom of God unless they are born of water and the Spirit. Flesh gives birth to flesh, but the Spirit gives birth to spirit. You should not be surprised at my saying, 'You must be born again.' The wind blows wherever it pleases. You hear its sound, but you cannot tell where it comes from or where it is going. So it is with everyone born of the Spirit."
>
> **John 3:5-8**

Jesus was not speaking of physical birth but of a birth of the spirit. Until there is a birth of spirit, the spirit is yet to be born. There is no future of a life eternal. Accepting Jesus as Lord of one's life breathes life into the spirit. This is being "born again" at the spiritual level and is required for the hope of eternal life with Him. If one dies without Jesus in his or her heart, there is a future eternity separated from God forever.

There are people who think they are too "far gone" to receive redemption. Some people I invited to church would say something to the effect: If I came to church, the roof would cave in. Not true. I have been in many churches and never once have I experienced a single cave-in. Nothing anyone has done is so bad that he cannot be forgiven. Judas betrayed Jesus and sold Him out for 30 pieces of silver (Matthew 26). As heinous as this was, if Judas had asked for forgiveness, God would have forgiven him.

Jesus died a horrible death nailed to a cross. Two criminals were also executed at the same time, one on each side of Him (Luke 23:32-43).

One criminal mocked Him while the other realized that He was the Son of God. That one asked Jesus to remember him. Jesus answered him, "Truly I tell you, today you will be with me in paradise" (Luke 23:43). Just before death, the one criminal believed in Jesus. This indicates that it is never too late for anyone. These two criminals represent everyone in the the world. There are those who accept and those who reject Jesus. Which criminal made the better choice?

The most important decision any of us will ever make in this life is what to do with Jesus. He is the key to doing more than just surviving. He wants people to have an abundant life (John 10:10). This does not necessarily mean that there will be an overabundance of material possessions. It does mean God promises to meet our needs and that there is a heavenly eternal home for those who trust in Him.

A New Command

God commands us to love one another. A command is not a suggestion. When a person in charge gives a command that person expects his people to comply.

> "A new command I give you: Love one another. As I have loved you, so you must love one another. By this everyone will know that you are my disciples, if you love one another."
>
> *John 13:34-35*

Three times in two verses Jesus tells His disciples to "love one another." Jesus was trying to express how important it is to love.

One of the teachers of the law debated Jesus, asking Him, "Of all the commandments, which is the most important" (Mark 12:28)? Jesus replied:

> "The most important one," answered Jesus, "is this: 'Hear, O Israel: The Lord our God, the Lord is one. Love the Lord your God with all your heart and with all your soul and with all your mind and with all your strength.' The second is this: 'Love your neighbor as yourself.' There is no commandment greater than these."
>
> *Mark 12:29-31*

Loving God is the core of this scripture. Loving Him is at the heart because He is the source of love. The only way to love others is to have a loving relationship with God. Think of it this way: Electricity supplies power to homes. Without electricity, life would be much more difficult. God is the electrical source of power that enables us to love others. Without the source of an unending supply of love, we cannot love others as we should. We obtain this love by our continual relationship with Him.

Learning to love others is central to the Christian faith. This is all goodness and light until we encounter those who are "more challenging." Some people are not easy to love. The Bible does not differentiate between the loveable and the not-so-loveable. Jesus taught us to love our enemies.

> "You have heard that it was said, 'Love your neighbor and hate your enemy.' But I tell you, love your enemies and pray for those who persecute you, that you may be children of your Father in heaven. He causes his sun to rise on the evil and the good, and sends rain on the righteous and the unrighteous. If you love those who love you, what reward will you get? Are not even the tax collectors doing that? And if you greet only your own people, what are you doing more than others? Do not even pagans do that? Be perfect, therefore, as your heavenly Father is perfect."

> ***Matthew 5:43-48***

Imagine a pill in the form of these verses. Could you "swallow" it? It is easy to love family and friends. Where the work begins is when the not so loveable enter the picture. They can come in the form of relatives, in-laws, people in the church, and co-workers. You know the type: No one can stand to be around them. How do we believers deal with these people? Per Jesus' words, His people should love and pray for them. He does not encourage associating with enemies or persecutors. All He says is to pray for and love them. Love for these people does not come naturally. Loving them comes from a heart filled with love from God. Only He can give this supernatural ability to love enemies.

Letting God fill a life with His love is a way to excel at surviving. Casting off past hurts and allowing God's love to fill these areas will free us from the chains that hinder. God's supernatural love will liberate us to survive anything life can throw at us.

To Think About:

1. When going through a difficult time, what are you doing to help yourself? Are you studying the Bible and reading other Christian books to deal with your situation?

2. Are you investing time in others?

3. Have you taken an honest look at yourself? Are any changes in order?

4. Is Jesus the true Lord of your life?

5. How are you doing at loving others? Is there room for improvement? Is there someone in your life you can reach out to in love or in prayer?

13 – There is a Pony in There

"...weeping may stay for the night, but rejoicing comes in the morning."

Psalm 30:5

D ire times lead to dark places. Some people say there is light at the end of the tunnel. But what if a person cannot even see the tunnel? Answers or even directions are difficult to unearth when groping in the dark. A dependable light source, Jesus, penetrates the obscurity. "The light shines in the darkness, and the darkness has not overcome it" (John 1:5). Darkness never overcomes light but only lasts until there is light. The smallest source of light in a dark room eliminates the darkness.

How do we find a light in difficult times? Jesus referred to Himself as Light. When Jesus spoke to the people he said, "I am the light of the world. Whoever follows me will never walk in darkness, but will have the light of life" (John 8:12). Jesus is the Light in dark times. He may not remove us from those times but He will surely guide us through them by lighting the way. In this way, He is indeed our Leading Light. "To this you were called, because Christ suffered for you, leaving you an example, that you should follow in his steps" (1 Peter 2:21). Peter speaks of suffering for doing what is good. Wrongdoing often brings punishment, but what if doing what is right brings punishment? Jesus had done no wrong, but received undeserved punishment and suffered terribly. Followers of Jesus should keep His example in mind when they are treated poorly for doing what is good.

Sometimes difficult situations last for years. It is like going through a horrific storm. There is wind, rain, and lightning, but eventually the storm passes. The sun comes out and a brighter day comes. The gloominess of the storm passes and sunshine fills the air.

Hope

What is hope? One dictionary defines hope as "a feeling that what is wanted will happen; desire accompanied by expectation."[9] Compare this to what the Bible says about hope. "Through him you believe in God, who raised him from the dead and glorified him, and so your faith and hope are in God" (1 Peter 1:21). Peter is speaking of Jesus raised from the dead and glorified.

Hope in the Bible is much more than the hope defined in dictionaries. The dictionary definition could refer to someone hoping to pass an exam in school. Biblical hope has different characteristics.

> For everything that was written in the past was written
> to teach us, so that through the endurance taught in
> the Scriptures and the encouragement they provide we
> might have hope.
>
> ### Romans 15:4

Paul offers hope in his writings. Remember, the Bible we know today did not exist when Paul wrote the book of Romans. The Scripture he referred to is found in what we call the Old Testament. We now have the writings of the New Testament in addition to the Old Testament, and both are sources of hope. Studying the Scriptures is necessary for finding the true hope revealed in God's Word.

In chapter nine, I stated that grace is an undeserved gift that God gives. Without grace, all of us stand condemned. God gives us His grace when we decide to follow Him and His Word. The grace that God gives frees us from our sins. Grace gives us hope in knowing we are no longer condemned for our sins.

---

9. *Webster's New World Dictionary,* Third College Edition (New York, NY: Simon & Schuster, Inc., 1988), p. 650.

The ultimate hope for the follower of Jesus is the promise of His return. Jesus ascended into Heaven (Luke 24:51) and He will return (Revelation 19:11-16).

> ...while we wait for the blessed hope—the appearing of the glory of our great God and Savior, Jesus Christ, who gave himself for us to redeem us from all wickedness and to purify for himself a people that are his very own, eager to do what is good.
>
> *Titus 2:13-14*

These are a few examples of the hope those who follow Jesus experience. Reading the Bible will unearth more aspects of the hope that God gives. When we place our hope in God, it will never fail. When our hope is misplaced or lost, however, we enter a place of bleakness and disillusionment. The only true and dependable hope is the hope God offers.

"Life is meaningless" is the main theme of the book of Ecclesiastes. The writer gives the impression that *life stinks...and then you die.* Then at the end of the book, he offers a profound view of the meaning of life.

> Now all has been heard; here is the conclusion of the matter: Fear God and keep his commandments, for this is the duty of all mankind. For God will bring every deed into judgment, including every hidden thing, whether it is good or evil.
>
> *Ecclesiastes 12:13-14*

The author of Ecclesiastes concludes that a relationship with God adds meaning to life and gives hope for the future.

Jesus went to the cross for all humanity. He shed His blood for all the sins of people. Up until Jesus willingly sacrificed Himself, atonement for peoples' sins came through animal sacrifice. When the Bible speaks of atonement as a payment for a penalty, it is like receiving a ticket for a traffic violation. A court assesses a fine, and the violator pays the fine. In the case of atonement, sin is the violation and a sacrifice is the payment of the fine. The shedding of animal blood covered the sins of the people, but the process had to be repeated because there was a continual need for atonement. Jesus took all sin upon Him – past, present, and future – and did away for the need for animal sacrifice once and for all. He took the punishment that belongs to all. People owed a fine for sin they could not pay, but Jesus paid it for them.

Those who believe in Jesus will not perish but have everlasting life (John 3:16). Jesus' death on the cross was not the end. His body lay in a tomb for three days. On the third day He rose from the dead just as He had said (Matthew 12:40).

What would the world be like if there were no hope? A world without hope is a scary thought. There are people who come to a certain period in their life when they can see no hope. There is nothing left for them. Some who have lost all hope decide that there is no other way out but to take their life.

Many people lose hope, which can take them into an even deeper darkness. The loss of hope clouds one's sight so that there is seemingly no way out of the lightless pit. The loss of hope tells a person there is no future and no purpose.

I responded to many suicide and attempted suicide calls during my police career. People at that moment have lost hope and can see no future. One incident in particular I will never forget. A retired officer who had been arrested took his life while in jail after one of his family members accused him of a crime. I had known this man since we attended the police academy together. After retirement, he studied to enter the pastorate. I was shocked when I heard the news and then received a further shock when the family member retracted the accusations after it was too late. What a senseless waste.

This is only one such tragic story among thousands across America. The Center for Disease Control and Prevention reports 41,149 suicides in the United States in 2013.[10] Although this number is staggering, it is likely lower than the actual number of suicides because statistics do not record all suicide deaths. For example, if someone intentionally drives

---

10. https://www.cdc.gov/violenceprevention/pdf/suicide-datasheet-a.pdf. Accessed September 19, 2016.

a car into a fixed object and dies, a possible suicide is categorized as an accident.

The sense of hopelessness leads to feelings of despair. Despair obscures rational thinking. The absence of rational thinking means there is a deficiency of good decision-making. A person who decides to take his or her life is not thinking clearly. Those who normally would never think of harming themselves do the "unthinkable" in the desperate darkness of hopelessness.

One day I asked Mortimer, the young pastor who took over the church plant and walked out of the service his last Sunday, "What happens if a person commits suicide?" His reply was, "They're going to hell." I was not surprised at his answer since that was his sermon topic every Sunday. I am afraid, however, that he is not the only person who believes this.

No specific passages in the Bible address or explain the issue of suicide. Some reason that taking one's own life is committing murder because suicide is self-murder. Since the Bible teaches that murder is wrong, suicide is a sin. Others have even taken the extreme position that suicide is an unpardonable sin.

The Bible records very few cases of suicide. Saul and his armor-bearer took their own lives (1 Samuel 31:4-6). Ahithophel hanged himself (2 Samuel 17:23). Judas, the betrayer of Jesus, hanged himself (Matthew 27:5).

Although the Bible is vague concerning suicide, several accounts depict those who have been through so much strife that they want to die. Elijah, a prophet, confronted the prophets of Baal and had them put to death (1 Kings 18). After this, Jezebel (one of the vilest women in all the Bible) sent a message to Elijah saying that she would have him killed (1 Kings 19:2).

> Elijah was afraid and ran for his life. When he came
> to Beersheba in Judah, he left his servant there, while
> he himself went a day's journey into the wilderness. He
> came to a broom bush, sat down under it and prayed
> that he might die. "I have had enough, Lord," he said.
> "Take my life; I am no better than my ancestors." Then
> he lay down under the bush and fell asleep.
>
> *1 Kings 19:3-5*

Elijah "had enough." He lived with the constant possibility of death while opposing false prophets, and now Jezebel wanted him dead. He was hungry, tired, and alone and viewed death as a relief. His story did not end under the broom bush. An angel came and gave him food and drink. He rested, regained his strength, and traveled 40 days to Horeb, referred to as "the mountain of God" (1 Kings 19:5-9).

Suicide is not a viable solution to life's ordeals. Life can certainly be physically and emotionally painful, and suicide is a way of ending the pain. But there is another consideration: Life is a gift from God. No matter how difficult the situation, it is not up to an individual to end life. That is God's decision – and His alone. He gave life and it is His to take. Ending one's life is saying, "I know what's better for me than God does." God alone sees the whole big picture. He can take the most difficult situations and turn them around for good. "And we know that in all things God works for the good of those who love him, who have been called according to his purpose" (Romans 8:28). Though it is not easy to see this when going through trials, it is the truth – God's truth on the matter of suffering and persevering through it.

No person can truly know how God thinks (1 Corinthians 2:11). Scripture gives us a hint of how God thinks, but His ways are not ours. He knows that someone who takes his or her life is not thinking properly. To say that committing suicide is an automatic sentence to hell is not only a simplistic answer but a wrong one. What makes suicide an unpardonable sin? Is it suicide for a police officer to place him or herself in a deadly situation? Was it suicide for Jesus to die willingly even though He could have stopped it at any moment? What happens when a follower of Jesus – one who by faith has trusted Him and received His free gift of grace – commits suicide? Does suicide invalidate that grace and bar him or her from spending eternity in Heaven? These questions need serious consideration before one pronounces judgment on someone who takes his life. One of my former police academy mates made a commitment to God and was preparing for ministry. At the moment when he took his life, he was not thinking properly. He saw this as the solution to his situation. Did this single decision in a single moment keep him from an eternal home?

Those who suspect that someone may be contemplating suicide must be diligent. Be aware of others' actions. Are there changes in behavior or is someone beginning to withdraw? Is he or she speaking in terms that suggest there is no reason to live? Be a good listener. If you suspect something is going on, ask the person directly: "Are you thinking about hurting or even killing yourself?" This question can save a life. If you have any suspicion, do not be afraid to ask.

If someone is contemplating suicide, take action. If possible, do not leave the person alone. As we see in the case of Elijah, being alone adds to the condition. See if there are local resources that deal with those who are thinking about taking their life. The *National Suicide Prevention Lifeline* (1-800-273-8255) is available 24/7. These are people trained to speak to those thinking of suicide. Getting help is an important step when a person is at the point of suicide.

Faith

There is a difference between faith and hope. One dictionary defines faith as "unquestioning belief in God, religious tenets, etc."[11] The Bible defines faith as "confidence in what we hope for and assurance about what we do not see" (Hebrews 11:1). Faith is belief in and trusting in an unseen God. Jesus said, "Because you have seen me, you have believed; blessed are those who have not seen and yet have believed" (John 20:29). Biblical faith is the belief in the unseen (God), and hope is an expectation of a future event.

One of my favorite illustrations of faith is the story of the centurion. Centurions were the "police" in Jesus' day. A centurion approached Jesus and explained that one of his servants was ill. Jesus asked the centurion if He should come and heal the servant. The centurion told Him that it was not necessary for Him to come to his home. The centurion told Jesus all He had to do was say the word and heal the servant. "When Jesus heard this, he was amazed and said to those following him, 'Truly I tell you, I have not found anyone in Israel with such great faith'" (Matthew 8:10). "Then Jesus said to the centurion, 'Go! Let it be done just as you believed it would.' And his servant was healed at that moment" (Matthew 8:13). All of us need to strive for faith like this centurion had.

---

11. *Webster's New World Dictionary*, Third College Edition (New York, NY: Simon & Schuster, Inc., 1988), p. 487.

A father with a demon-possessed son asked Jesus' disciples for help, but they could not heal the boy. The man then took the boy to Jesus who healed the boy immediately. The disciples asked Jesus why they were unable to heal the boy.

> He replied, "Because you have so little faith. Truly I tell you, if you have faith as small as a mustard seed, you can say to this mountain, 'Move from here to there,' and it will move. Nothing will be impossible for you."
>
> *Matthew 17:20-21*

The Bible refers to a mustard seed as "the smallest of seeds on earth" (Mark 4:31). Jesus was telling His disciples that it does not require a lot of faith to accomplish what He did when he healed the boy. The disciples were new to what Jesus was teaching them. Though they were with Jesus, they had the same struggles that we have today. We cannot fault them for their apparent deficiency in faith. Everyone has issues around faith at one time or another. What is important is that they stayed with Jesus and continued to grow in faith.

When Jesus used the illustration of the mustard seed, He was saying that it does not take a lot of faith to accomplish His work. A mustard seed is very small but when planted grows large.

> Then Jesus asked, "What is the kingdom of God like? What shall I compare it to? It is like a mustard seed, which a man took and planted in his garden. It grew and became a tree, and the birds perched in its branches."
>
> *Luke 13:18-19*

This illustration can also apply to faith. Initially faith begins just like the mustard seed. As time passes, faith continues to grow. People nurture faith by prayer, reading God's Word, and practicing obedience.

Dictionaries define "faith" as a noun. A noun refers to a person, place, or thing. There is no action involved. For those who are followers of Jesus, faith needs to be a verb. A verb puts a noun to work, adding action to a person's faith.

What good is it, my brothers and sisters, if someone claims to have faith but has no deeds? Can such faith save them? Suppose a brother or a sister is without clothes and daily food. If one of you says to them, "Go in peace; keep warm and well fed," but does nothing about their physical needs, what good is it? In the same way, faith by itself, if it is not accompanied by action, is dead.

James 2:14-17

James holds that faith without action is dead. Picture yourself in a rowboat in the middle of a lake. You need to get to shore before it gets dark. There are two oars in the boat. What are you going to do? Are you going to just sit there in the boat believing you will get to the shore safe and sound, or are you going to put the oars in their mounts and row to shore before darkness comes? The boat represents faith. The oars represent works. The boat will not move until the oars are in action. In biblical teaching, faith and action cannot work independent of one another. Anyone can have faith. That faith minus action, however, is not faith as defined in the Bible. Biblical faith includes the component of action. Faith must be a verb.

Priorities

Our priorities change as life progresses. In the younger years, our priorities are school and friends. Later, it's marriage and an occupation. When we start a family, children become a priority. One priority should never change – the priority of God in one's life. God should never be anywhere but first.

In Luke 10, Jesus and the disciples went to a village, and Martha opened her home to them. This was not Jesus' first visit to this home. He stayed there often while in Jerusalem. Jesus knew Mary and her siblings well, which explains why Martha felt comfortable enough to share her grievances with Jesus. This scene is like one from a typical family setting. One sister feels that the other is not doing her share of the work.

Martha's sister Mary decided to sit at the feet of Jesus instead of helping Martha with all the preparations. Martha went to Jesus and said,

"Lord, don't you care that my sister has left me to do the work by myself? Tell her to help me!" You can see Martha's attitude. She was probably thinking, "why am I doing all this while my lazy sister is lounging at the feet of Jesus?" This was not an issue of a lazy sister but an issue of priorities. Martha chose to begin doing the work, which took her time – time she could have spent with Jesus. Mary, on the other hand, chose to sit and spend time with Jesus. What was Jesus' response to Martha?

> "Martha, Martha," the Lord answered, "you are worried and upset about many things, but few things are needed—or indeed only one. Mary has chosen what is better, and it will not be taken away from her."

> **Luke 10:41-42**

Which sister made the better choice? Jesus' response to Martha shows that Mary made the better choice. Though Martha perhaps thought she was doing the right thing in showing hospitality to their guest, her priorities were not right. Mary probably ended up helping Martha, but Mary chose to take time out and spend it with Jesus first. Mary put Jesus ahead of the busyness in the home.

What is the lesson in this story? The lesson we should learn is about priorities. In saying "yes" to one thing we say "no" to something else. Martha said "yes" to work, which said "no" to spending time with Jesus. Mary said "yes" to spending time with Jesus, which said "no" to helping her sister Martha. Keep this in mind when you are deciding how you will spend your time or making any choice to do something: Saying "yes" to doing one thing is saying "no" to another.

If the "busyness" of life prevents us from spending time with Jesus, then our priorities need adjusting. If God does not take first place, do not expect things to go as well as they could. Not making God a priority is saying that a person knows more than God does. Think about this: Not taking time out for God every day is saying, "I have no need for God." When you have no interaction with God to seek Him for help and guidance, you are saying, "I got this. I can do this on my own."

A popular bumper sticker declared: "God is My Co-Pilot." If God is the "co-pilot," then the seating arrangement needs changing. If God is not the pilot of your life, your priorities are wrong. Being a follower of Jesus implies a life in submission to Him. So if we confess that we are followers of Jesus, our lives must be in alignment with God and His Word.

Consider the need for wheel alignment in vehicles. To work and wear properly, tires must be in proper alignment. If they are not, tires will wear out sooner and the car will not steer correctly. A car out of alignment tends to veer to one side or the other and does not go straight. The same applies to a person's life. If our lives are not in proper alignment with God, it will be a struggle for us to stay on the road that God has mapped out.

Making God a priority also means making God the Lord of our finances. This is a touchy subject. I have heard it said so many times that "all these churches want is money." The question one might pose is: "How are churches to function without money?" How is any ministry to function without money? People who have an issue with churches' needing money most likely have an issue with money. I heard a pastor say, "Show me someone's checkbook and I will tell where their heart is." The checkbook is a compass of the heart. Where the money goes is where the heart is. God's Word deals with how we should view money.

> No one can serve two masters. Either you will hate the one and love the other, or you will be devoted to the one and despise the other. You cannot serve both God and money.
>
> ### *Matthew 6:24*

Money by itself is not bad; the *love* of money makes it bad (1 Timothy 6:10). Anytime something becomes more of a priority than God, it becomes sin. The word for placing something above God in importance is "idolatry," or the worship of idols. Many things become idols. Money has the potential to become a sin. How can money become sin? If someone places the importance of money over the importance of God, money – the so-called "almighty dollar" – has become an idol to that person.

Money comes from God in the first place. Who gave a person the ability to earn money? God's people should develop a discipline of giving. The priority of giving should be to the church one attends. The standard is usually 10% of one's income, which is called a tithe, which means tenth. In the Bible, people gave 10% of what they produced to the Lord. This is the basis for giving 10%. Giving is hard to master if there is not enough money to make ends meet. When the checkbook is bleeding red ink, we tend to hold back and not give to God what belongs to Him. Holding back in finances indicates a lack of trust that God will provide. Giving back to God is an act of faith. This is a stepping out of a comfort zone and saying to God, "I trust You with my finances."

> Remember this: Whoever sows sparingly will also reap sparingly, and whoever sows generously will also reap generously. Each of you should give what you have decided in your heart to give, not reluctantly or under compulsion, for God loves a cheerful giver.
>
> *1 Corinthians 9:6-7*

Give Thanks

The Bible teaches us to give thanks in all circumstances (1 Thessalonians 5:18). Giving thanks in the good times is easier than in the bad. Being thankful is simple when the pantry and refrigerator are full of food. But being thankful is hard when a hungry person does not know where the next meal is coming from.

Jesus taught us to give thanks. Before eating together with His disciples, He gave thanks (Matthew 26:26). Though having bread to eat may not seem significant, we need to be thankful in *all* things. We come to expect many things rather than appreciate them. This is true in many areas of life: personal, relational, and material.

Good friendships are blessings to cherish. The quality of friendship matters. "One who has unreliable friends soon comes to ruin, but there is a friend who sticks closer than a brother" (Proverbs 18:24). On social media, people take pride in having many friends. Out of those hundreds of "friends," however, there is little contact or closeness.

> I no longer call you servants, because a servant does not
> know his master's business. Instead, I have called you
> friends, for everything that I learned from my Father I
> have made known to you.

> *John 15:15*

Jesus calls His people friends. This indicates the importance of friendship. True friends can keep a confidence and are dependable. Give thanks for the blessing of one or two close and trustworthy friends because good friends are hard to find.

I learned to be more thankful for what I have during my trials. I did not realize how little I was giving thanks. Now I give thanks daily for the things I have. I thank God every day for the food on my table, the socks on my feet, the gas in my tank, and the air that I breathe. Thanking God for everything has changed me. It has made me more appreciative of the things I have and reduced my worry about the things I do not have. This is especially true for the people in my life. Giving thanks is life changing.

Good Fruit

I think most people appreciate a good piece of fruit. Fruit fresh off the tree is hard to top. Another fruit that cannot be beat is the fruit described in the Bible, the fruit of the Spirit.

> But the fruit of the Spirit is love, joy, peace, forbearance,
> kindness, goodness, faithfulness, gentleness and self-
> control. Against such things there is no law.

> *Galatians 5:22-23*

Some Christians seem to think that showing the fruit of the Spirit means they must look like someone sucking on a sour lemon. A well-known artist's interpretation of Jesus portrays Him laughing. This side of Jesus often goes unnoticed. Jesus was also human and experienced the same feelings and emotions we all do. Laughing coincides with scripture: "A cheerful heart is good medicine, but a crushed spirit dries up the bones" (Proverbs 17:22). Laughter is medicine for the soul. I love getting together with people who like to laugh and have a good time. Laughing is contagious. Try to associate with people who are not afraid to laugh. Associating with positive people will also be beneficial when you are going through hard times. Chances are, these people have had troubles in life, too, but have learned that laughter is good medicine.

Some older movies portray Jesus as a blue-eyed man with a beard and long brown hair clad in a long white robe. The actor cast as Jesus displayed no emotion regardless of the situation Jesus was facing. He looked as if he had taken an illicit drug. This portrayal of Jesus is not what He is truly like. When Jesus was sitting around a fire at night and talking with friends, there was laughter.

Jesus used hyperbole, an exaggeration to make a point, in many of His illustrations. He commented about removing the plank out of your own eye before getting the speck of sawdust out of your brother's eye (Matthew 7:3-5). Think of having a 10-foot long 2x4 plank in your eye while telling someone else they have a small speck of sawdust! This was a humorous way of telling people not to be so critical of others. Jesus also knew that it is much easier to see the faults in others than in oneself.

There is a "time to weep and a time to laugh" (Ecclesiastes 3:4). When going through a difficult time no one feels like laughing. Laughing in the middle of a messy situation is laughing at an inopportune time and may be a way of covering what is going on in a person's life. There is laughter on the outside but sadness on the inside. In time, genuine laughter will come.

Good Fear, Bad Fear

The Bible references the word fear over 300 times. Some references deal with a healthy fear of God and others are warnings not to fear. Fear can overwhelm a person confronted with challenging situations. As a police officer, I was in numerous situations where my life was in jeopardy. In each situation, I made a conscious decision that no matter what took place, I would trust that God had me in His hands. I was still afraid, which is a very human and logical response. What I am saying is that I did not allow fear to overwhelm me. Fear can paralyze if allowed to do so. God wants us to live fearlessly. How are we to live a life without fear?

God is love. Whoever lives in love lives in God, and God in them. This is how love is made complete among us so that we will have confidence on the day of judgment: In this world we are like Jesus. There is no fear in love. But perfect love drives out fear, because fear has to do with punishment. The one who fears is not made perfect in love.

1 John 4:16-18

John says there is no fear if we are living in love. Perfect love drives out fear. This love manifests in believers as they mature, and as it does it drives out fear.

What is the difference between good and bad fear? The Bible speaks of the fear of God and the fear of man. "Do not be afraid of those who kill the body but cannot kill the soul. Rather, be afraid of the One who can destroy both soul and body in hell" (Matthew 10:28). The one who can kill the body but not the soul is man. The One who can kill both body and soul is God.

David, who became king over Judah (2 Samuel 2), had humble beginnings as a shepherd. Tending sheep kept him away from people, and most did not know who he was. God told Samuel the prophet to anoint David because God had a purpose for him. Not long after this, the Philistines were preparing for war against Judah (1 Samuel 17). A nine-foot tall giant of a being named Goliath came out of the Philistine camp and began taunting Israel's army. He challenged anyone to step out and fight him so he could kill them. This taunting went on for 40 days, and no one from the camp of Israel took the challenge. Finally, David rose to the challenge to fight Goliath. David selected stones to use in his sling. He was well-versed in using a sling because he used it to protect his flock. So he approached the giant and loaded his sling. As the giant moved closer, David flung the stone with such force that the rock was buried in Goliath's forehead. Goliath fell facedown to the ground and died that day (1 Samuel 17:48-51).

The story of David is an example of the fear of man versus the fear of God. Not one of the battle-hardened soldiers in the army of Israel dared face Goliath, who was humiliating their nation and honor. Seeing how big he was, no one even considered facing him on the battlefield. David was an unlikely hero if ever there was one. He was no soldier but a young tender of sheep and no match for the seasoned giant of a warrior. Yet David stepped forward. What was the difference between David and the others in Israel? David knew his God was bigger than any giant. His confidence was not in a sling or a rock but in Almighty God. That is what separated him from the others. He had made the distinction between the fear of man and the fear of God.

The difference in these two aspects of fear is that man can only kill the body and has no control over the destiny of the soul. God has control over both body and soul. He determines where the soul spends eternity. The fear of a fellow human being is misplaced fear. The only fear we should have is a reverent fear of God.

Perseverance

When you are going through difficult times, remember that God is preparing you for what He has planned. God has a plan for everyone. The only condition is that a person must seek it. God will reveal what He has in store when the appropriate time comes.

> As you know, we count as blessed those who have persevered. You have heard of Job's perseverance and have seen what the Lord finally brought about. The Lord is full of compassion and mercy.
>
> *James 5:11*

Perseverance through hard times conditions you for the future. When we persevere, we become stronger in hope and faith.

Physical strength is subject to failure. What is more important than the physical is the spiritual. Spiritual strength continues to grow throughout a lifetime. "Never be lacking in zeal, but keep your spiritual fervor, serving the Lord" (Romans 12:11). Though the body will fail, the spiritual aspect of life will not. People are spiritual beings having a human experience. The spirit is going to live forever. Your spiritual fervor is a light and witness to others. Keep that light lit at all times.

During the Olympics, we witness the endurance of long-distance runners. These competitors spend hours covering the 26.2-mile distance of a marathon. They must pace themselves to make it all the way to the finish line. This is also true in a spiritual sense when following Jesus. To endure to the end one must pace him or herself.

The goal in this life should be to run the "race" well. There will be bumps and potholes along the way. This race is not a sprint but a marathon. The proper pace in a marathon is essential for finishing the race. Those who follow Jesus are all winners. There is no first or last place. All that is required is to finish the race. The Apostle Paul stated it well shortly before his execution.

> For I am already being poured out like a drink offering, and the time for my departure is near. I have fought the good fight, I have finished the race, I have kept the faith. Now there is in store for me the crown of righteousness, which the Lord, the righteous Judge, will award to me on that day—and not only to me, but also to all who have longed for his appearing.
>
> *2 Timothy 4:6-8*

Paul was in a Roman prison for the second time and knew that he was not likely to be released. His words should be an inspiration to us. Our desire should be to echo these words when our race is complete: *I have fought the good fight, I have finished the race, I have kept the faith.* On the other side of the finish line is a loving God who will greet His people with open arms.

The Pony in the Manure Pile

I would like to report that after going through all the manure, I have found a new love of my life. Sounds good for a fairy tale ending, but it is not that simple. These experiences have allowed me to grow. My faith and trust in God have grown. My love and care for others have grown. I am more patient when dealing with people. The laboring through the manure has helped produce growth.

Some have experienced much worse than I have. But we must recognize the common thread that binds us together: We all experience many of the same challenges and sufferings. No person is exempt from trials in this life. At times we will be knee deep in manure. Like the two boys in the story at the beginning of the book, we can look at it two different ways. We may only see the pile of manure or we can look for the pony.

We can merely survive or we can strive for a better life. We do not have to live in bitterness and unforgiveness. The choice is ours, and we do not need to just "get through" life alone. God is there, and He has a plan for everyone. A person must reach out to Him and accept what He offers. Though it is not easy to see and is sometimes difficult to understand, it is the best for us.

We form most of our view of the world at an early age. When we decide to follow Jesus, no matter how young or old we are, He rewrites the prescription for our worldview lenses. Our vision changes gradually, and Jesus continually readjusts our lenses. The changing view allows us to see much differently than before. When we look through these new eyeglasses, we have more love and compassion for others. This new "eyesight" allows us to look past the exterior – unlike a world that is so focused on the exterior and not the heart of a person. People begin to matter more and we see that *all* people have value.

Our past does not define us; a relationship with God does. But we must ask God into our life. That is not an easy proposition when we have been running our own life. Comparing this life to eternity gives us a very different perspective on this life. Some people live past 100 years of age, but contrasting that with the forever of eternity makes that 100 years seem minuscule. The question we need to ponder is: "Where am I going after this life is over?" This is the most important question for us to pose, and the answer is literally a matter of life and death. We can either be with God eternally or be separated from Him forever.

The writer of Ecclesiastes wrestles with the meaning of life. Why are we here on this earth? The book opens, "'Meaningless! Meaningless!' says the Teacher. Utterly meaningless! Everything is meaningless" (Ecclesiastes 1:1). Thus toils in this life have no meaning. The writer struggles with the question, "Is there purpose and meaning to life?"

If we are honest, we all have dealt with this fight at one time or another: Is there purpose? Is there meaning? The writer concludes there is no meaning or purpose apart from a relationship with God (Ecclesiastes 12: 9-14). A personal relationship with our Creator is the key to meaning and purpose.

We only get one chance at this life. There are no do-overs or mulligans. How we live determines the outcome. More importantly, how we answer the question of Jesus will determine the ending. The two criminals crucified with Jesus reveal the difference in responses. One criminal accepted Jesus before he died, and the other rejected Him. Jesus promised one that he would be with Him in paradise while the other was eternally separated (Luke 23:43).

Sometimes we cannot understand that the God of the Bible loves us no matter what we have done. God's love for people is like an ever-flowing fountain of living water. All we need to do is come to this fountain and drink. We must invite God into our heart, where He will come in and reside.

The resurrected Jesus is the hope for all. He suffered and died to save everyone – *every one*. From what did Jesus save us? He saved us from the punishment we deserve by dying in our place. Jesus not only died but overcame death so all may live. When life as we know it ceases, it is not an end but a beginning for those who follow Jesus. There is victory over death.

The name of the pony in the manure pile is Victory. No matter how messy life gets, there will be light at the end of the tunnel. There is light in the darkness. That Light is Jesus. God gives the victory. We can endure intense circumstances and terrifying trials without end. Yet there is victory in all situations. Jesus conquered death by dying on a cross and leaving behind an empty tomb. God, through His Son, Jesus Christ, gives victory to those who follow Him.

"But thanks be to God! He gives us the victory through our Lord Jesus Christ."

1 Corinthians 15:57

www.ingramcontent.com/pod-product-compliance
Lightning Source LLC
LaVergne TN
LVHW011204080426
835508LV00007B/594